THE WAY OF HAIKU

THE WAY OF HAIKU

Naomi Beth Wakan

Shanti Arts Publishing
Brunswick, Maine

THE WAY OF HAIKU

Published by Shanti Arts Publishing
Cover and interior design by Shanti Arts Designs

Shanti Arts LLC
193 Hillside Road
Brunswick, Maine 04011

www.shantiarts.com

Cover image by Christine Brooks Cote
and used with her permission.

All haiku are printed with permission of the authors;
in the event of an oversight, please contact the author
or publisher and proper acknowledgment will be
made in forthcoming editions. Poems not attributed
are by Naomi Beth Wakan. Crow Haiga by Carole
MacRury is gratefully used with her permission.

Printed in the United States of America

ISBN: 978-1-947067-67-7 (softcover)
ISBN: 978-1-947067-68-4 (ebook)

Library of Congress Control Number: 2018964699

To the members of pacifi-kana haiku group, with special thanks to Michael Dylan Welch, Alice Frampton, Vicki McCullough, Terry Ann Carter, and Carole MacRury for their caring support.

Mindfulness is knowing what's happening, while it's happening, without preference or judgment.

— ROB NAIRN

Haiku are transmitters of the smallest manageable element of insight.

— WWW.TNELLEN.COM

He who aspires to be a great poet must first become a little child.

— MACAULAY

Don't follow in the footsteps of the old poets, seek what they sought.

— BASHŌ

Outside of truth there is no poetry.
Makoto no hoka ni haikai nashi

— UEJIMA ONITSURA

CONTENTS

INTRODUCTION

THE WEB IS OVERFLOWING WITH USEFUL ESSAYS ON haiku—how to write them, how to read them, their history, their present state, their future.

The information they provide is overwhelming and confusing. In *The Way of Haiku*, I am writing for absolute beginners, introducing readers to the basics of haiku, as well as a few subtleties, and directing them to sites and books that can take them in deeper. This book is a foretaste, an hors d'oeuvre as it were, just enough to whet the appetite, but also enough to help the reader continue on to the main course and the rest of the meal.

Writing haiku has changed my life in so many ways: it has kept me grounded in the here and now, it has helped me to focus my words into an intensity that I didn't know words could have, and it has introduced me to a world of *haijin* (haiku writers).These wonderful haijin not only have the ability to hit the target in their own haiku, but they have been generous with their offerings of advice to further my own path. I hope this small book will help further yours.

WHAT IS HAIKU?

A RECENT CHECK ON THE WEB LISTED OVER TWENTY-NINE million entries for the word "haiku" (haiku covers both the singular and plural form) and over eight million for the word "sonnet." How is it possible that this small alien form of poetry has wormed its way into our hearts and into our reference sites, even exceeding the reference numbers for a type of verse firmly grounded in the Western tradition? And just what is haiku anyway?

Harold G. Henderson states that no two Japanese would quite agree on exactly what constitutes a haiku. Indeed the definitions range from haiku being considered purely literary efforts to haiku representing supreme moments of Zen awakening, with haiku as socio-cultural items being somewhere in between. As the definition field seems wide open, I might as well step immediately into an arena where angels fear to tread and attempt to define haiku — those brief poems that seem so easy to write and yet turn out to be so difficult that Bashō, the master of haiku, claimed to have written only ten good ones in a lifetime of writing. As befits a haijin, however, I will first give a deep Japanese bow and defer to older and definitely wiser (and some deceased) poets, letting them state their definitions before I offer mine. If the haiku writers that I quote from are unfamiliar to you, a list of these haiku personalities is at the back of the book.

Bashō, the father of haiku, said that "haiku is a flash of insight. What is happening in this place, at this moment." To this he added rather cryptically, "If you want to learn about the pine, go to the pine. If you want to learn about the bamboo, go to the bamboo." What can I say about this advice? Only that when the skin between you and the object dissolves (again turning to Bashō), "when you and the object become one, your poetry issues of its own accord." The fusion with the object allows the object to express its own qualities rather than have external projections put on it by the poet.

To see things as they are in the here and now seems to be an important haiku element. As Robert Spiess so neatly defines it: "The whole of life is in each moment, not in the past, not in the future, and thus a true haiku is virtually important because it is a moment of total genuine awareness of the reality of the Now." Ishikawa Takuboku, although writing about tanka, also understood the importance of capturing the moment when he said, "Although a sensation may last only a second, it is a second that will never return again. I refuse to let such moments slip by."

Haiku link all people by the use of seasonal images, but the exact image chosen . . . well, that depends on the individual poet. By using a familiar seasonal image, poets, if they capture the moment with intensity, can link their moment to all moments.

Again, accentuating the moment, Jim Kacian quotes an unnamed writer who states, "the poem should vanish . . . leaving us holding the moment it describes."

Now for R. H. Blyth, who wrote many volumes on haiku and almost single-handedly delivered this poetry form onto the English-speaking stage: "A haiku is the expression of a temporary enlightenment, in which we see into the life of things." He also stated, "Haiku does not aim at beauty. Like the music of Bach, it aims at significance, and some kind of beauty is found hovering near."

Temporary enlightenment . . . well, that was all the rage in the years after the Second World War when Zen swept into California and beyond. Jane Reichhold, however, pleaded for a less ambitious definition of haiku, so let's start with a few basics from Japan.

A traditional haiku, for the Japanese, is a poem of 5, 7, 5 phonetic sounds respectively, focused on a season and one particular moment within the season. Because of this, haiku are always written in the present tense, even if they are recording a moment long gone. The emotion of the moment is suggested by the described scene that stimulated it.

Harold G. Henderson put these ideas together and defined haiku as "a record of a moment of emotion in which human nature is somehow linked to all nature." He expands this by making the judgment that "all haiku worthy of the name are records of high moments — higher at least than the surrounding plain." Well, that seems a more modest demand than requesting it be a *satori* (enlightenment) moment every time. Just because haiku allow you to appreciate the briefness of life, they don't necessarily demand a Zen enlightenment experience before they can be written.

While we should not demand a satori moment in order to write haiku, neither should haiku be just an intellectual exercise recording something that we have noticed. Ishida Hakyō announced, "Haiku is not intellect, rather it is flesh

. . . haiku is not literature, haiku is raw life . . . composing haiku is synonymous with living life." Clark Strand also points out, "a haiku is not a photograph, it is a poem." Form aids the process of transforming the image into a poem, and while Henderson muses on the future form of haiku in English, he too points out that "a haiku is a poem and not a dribble of prose."

Daisetz Suzuki tries to cram a large number of aspects into his exploration of what a haiku is. "A haiku is the shortest form of poetry we can find in world literature. It consists of seventeen syllables [sic] into which have been cast some of the highest feelings human beings are capable of." Suzuki continues, "At the supreme moment of life and death we just utter a cry or take to action, we never argue, we never give ourselves up to lengthy talk. Feelings refuse to be conceptually dealt with, and a haiku is not the product of intellection. Hence its brevity and significance."

These are high ambitions for what is considered second-class poetry by poets of longer forms. Because so many people try to write haiku, particularly in Japan, where literally millions of people participate in haiku groups and competitions, haiku is often deemed a second-class form of poetry. This opinion is mostly declared by academic elitists who feel they have to set the standards for poetic excellence and that few will achieve these standards. Forget them! Haiku is a democratic poetry form. You don't need any kind of special knowledge to write haiku; you just need to see things clearly. Haiku-writing is as valid a way of expressing deep and condensed images as any other form of poetry.

The excellent Canadian haijin George Swede suggests that the following characteristics should be present in haiku: "brief; express a sense of awe, or transcendent insight; involve some aspect of nature (other than human); possess sense images; and present an event as happening now." He felt that the "Zen-like focus on the here and now" was the most telling of these criteria. And to quote him again, "it [haiku] is to glimpse the world that is related to beings, to nature or to the world where human beings and nature are living together, and there is a highly perceptive juxtaposition."

So here we are introduced to another haiku element: *toriawase* (the juxtaposition). Haiku usually include two images, the juxtaposition of which presents both images in a fresh light. The juxtaposition is accentuated by a break in the haiku. One-sentence haiku without the break are rarely successful, I feel.

For many people the break is the essence of haiku. It is the break that causes us to pause and let the essence of the haiku come through. From the pause comes the unsaid. In Japanese, the break is indicated by *kireji* (cutting words), which we'll take a more detailed look at later. The break accentuates the two images — nature and human nature juxtaposed, paralleled, or contrasted. However, the juxtaposition demands a segue, a connection between the two parts of the haiku. Speaking of the images, Patricia Donegan draws an interesting parallel when she states that "there needs to be two electric poles between which a spark leaps for the haiku to be effective; otherwise it is just a brief statement." Here are two spark-leaping haiku:

harusame ya
hachi no su tsutau
yane no mori

spring rain
follows the bee's nest
leaking through the roof

— Bashō, translated by Susumu Takiguchi

mihotoke no
okao no shimi ya
aki no ame

on the Buddha's
lofty face some spots
autumn rain

— Murakami Kijō

We don't usually associate a bee's nest with spring rain, nor spots with Buddha's face, yet here the images are beautifully linked.

The juxtaposition can be accentuated by use of the *kakekotoba* (pivot word or pivot line). These work in two different ways. The pivot word is usually a pun that can connect the first image of the haiku — using one meaning of the chosen homonym — with the second image — using the second meaning of the word. For example, here the word "fork" is used to mean a division as well as a piece of cutlery:

a sign
at the fork in the road
"fine dining"

— Jane Reichhold

As Sam Hamill points out, this double meaning introduces the ambiguity of much of Zen philosophy. The pivot line does not need to depend on a pun, however, but can merely be used to complete the image in the first line as well as introduce the image in the third, thus linking the two images. For example:

white on white roses
on her wedding day
her face pale
　　—Angelika Kolompar

The depth of perception that George Swede speaks of is accentuated by Patricia Donegan when she talks of the *hon-i* aspect of haiku, which she defines as "the way to call the spirit of the thing named." She points out that tanka, the precursor of haiku, are chanted rather than recited and originated in "spells and chants to invoke the deity." She wonders whether that power lingers on in haiku. Others, too, have suggested that through the *kigo* (seasonal word), which we will speak of later, haiku has direct links back to the shaman and the words he would call out to summon the nature spirits.

Robert Hass also speaks of haiku as "magical and ritual accounts of the Japanese year," and this definition again places accentuation on the season about which the haiku is being written and also on the linking of haiku back through *waka* (an earlier name for tanka) to the earliest form of Japanese poetry — incantations to the gods. Whether haijin are communicating with the gods is open for discussion. However, by identifying with the moment, haijin are able to efface themselves and allow a clearer kind of "seeing" to occur, a heightened awareness. *Makoto* is the word for this in Japanese, and like most Japanese words embedded deep in their culture, it is inadequate to translate it simply as "sincerity," but that will have to do for the moment. David Cobb describes makoto as "the truth of the poet's heart."

Insight does seem to be a key characteristic of haiku, as Kazuo Sato expresses it, "Haiku is a poetry of 'ahness' because it makes you say, 'Ah, now I see!'"

Michael Dylan Welch, a well known haiku writer and promoter of everything haiku, defined haiku this way for *Poets Market, 2005*: "Haiku is typically a three-line poem that uses concrete sensory images to convey or imply natural and human seasonal phenomena, using a two-part juxtapositional structure as well as simple and primarily objective language. Originally a Japanese genre of poetry, now written and adapted in many languages worldwide, traditional haiku in Japanese consists of seventeen phonetic sounds (not to be confused with syllables) in a pattern of 5, 7, 5. Because of differences in language, this rhythm is generally not followed for literary haiku in most languages other than Japanese. As intuitive and emotional poems, haiku often capture a sense of wonder and wholeness in presenting existence such as it is. Rather than presenting one's emotions, haiku present the cause of one's emotions, thus empowering the reader to have the same intuitive reaction to an experience that the poet had."

Well, that does rather say it all, but still, here's my rather modest offering: "Haiku are small verses, centered in the here and now, thus often including a seasonal reference, that present juxtaposed images in a way that opens the moment described to a deeper depth of understanding, not just of that particular moment, but of all moments in space and time."

HAIKU COUNT

THE FORM OF TRADITIONAL HAIKU IN JAPANESE IS 5, 7, 5 Japanese phonetic sounds. The phonetic sounds are usually rendered in English with two letters (e.g., ka, ki, ku, ke, ko), some with three (e.g., kya, kyu,), the vowels with one (a, i, u, e, o), and the letter "n." The phonetic sounds are not parallel to English syllables.

Haiku in the Japanese tradition are usually written vertically, starting from the right side of the page. Sometimes, if the haiku has accompanying illustrations, the poems are written as one long line to allow room for the painting.

I like Uchida Sono's comments on "the tight music of its seventeen sounds. A little longer and it becomes verbose; a little shorter and it loses its rhythm." But how to achieve that in English?

In English haiku, three lines is the most common form, with the second line usually being longer than the other two. Haiku in four lines or two lines, written vertically down the page, diagonally across it, or written horizontally in one line variously appear. I have also seen haiku written in three words, or even two, and once, only one word.

I find Ruth Yarrow's haiku, though brief, so profound that it leaves me gasping — and all in one line:

after the garden party   the garden

LeRoy Gorman offers something unexpected and clever:

> spring
> th
> awe
> her
> zip
> purr

Here Alexey Andreyev leaves me a little puzzled, although I could extemporize on stars winking, lovers winking, lover's moon . . . :

> moon
> wink

And then there is Cor van der Heuvel's famous one word haiku:

> tundra

What is this wide variety of haiku form all about?

As Norman Talbot says, "A short flat string of words with no obvious structure, no kigo (seasonal word), no kireji (cutting word), may flatter the elite who've seen it all before, but it does nothing for the simple, direct spirits that haiku used to be expected to awaken, awe, and refresh."

Clark Strand has a firm Zen meditation foundation for his haiku writing and so prefers to keep the 5, 7, 5 phonetic sounds of Japanese rule as a structure on which to hang his haiku. Just as the counting of the breath cuts out the discursive mind in meditation, so, he feels, the 5, 7, 5 phonetic sounds set a form to allow room for the haiku to manifest fully. Kaneko Tōta, although speaking of haiku written in Japanese rather than English, also supports this view with a similar comparison: "The 5, 7, 5 phonetic sound pattern provides a poetic framework for a poet in the same way that an established religion provides a moral framework for a man."

Clark Strand also points out that when you have counted out the phonetic sounds on your fingers and chosen a kigo (seasonal word), you have touched the mind of Bashō. I don't feel Bashō's mind was that limited, and as for me, I feel much closer to him when the old "Aha" hits my heart. But Strand's point is well taken.

Some haijin refuse to be trapped in form and rules. Susumu Takiguchi, founder and president of the World Haiku Club, states firmly, "The haiku poet writes the poem from the heart first, and looks to see if it has followed any principle second. To put up any haiku principle first and then force the work to follow it is an enticing trap which many fall into. My one and only principle in writing haiku is not to have any principles." Hino Sōjō supports this view with, "In my opinion, faithfulness to principle should give way to faithfulness to oneself."

As I mentioned, a Japanese phonetic sound often consists of only two letters. For this reason, the 5, 7, 5 rule can't be automatically transferred to a language such as English, where a syllable can be eight letters long; for example, "strength." The word for blue in Japanese is *aoi* and is counted as three phonetic sounds: a-o-i. Japanese is a heavily vowelled language, whereas English words have a paucity of vowels. Knightsbridge, a thirteen-letter word, has only three vowels, one of which is silent, yet consists of only two syllables. A Japanese haiku of 5, 7, 5 *on* (the Japanese word for a phonetic sound) therefore provides much less information than would a haiku of seventeen syllables written in English.

English is a stressed language, so haijin writing in English often choose Blyth's usage of three lines of two beats, three beats, two beats, and many times not even that, just three lines of blank verse. The three lines allow for the pause that traditionally comes after the fifth or the twelfth phonetic sound in Japanese haiku, which, in English can come after the first or second line.

What form is open to the writer of haiku then depends very much on how helpful they find a structure in stimulating their creativity. Possibilities can be seen to lie along a continuum from a strict, tight traditional structure to more and more anarchic forms. However, it's worth remembering, as Patricia Donegan says, "Haiku is an experience, not an act of counting syllables." Haiku is bigger than just syllable counting.

HOW TO WRITE HAIKU

I FEEL THAT HAIKU, LIKE PIXIES, DO NOT APPEAR ON demand. You have to be occupied elsewhere (not just idly doing something else, but really engrossed)—in weeding, being aware of the soles of your feet while walking, collecting shells on the beach, doing laundry. Only then will a haiku come through. You can long to create a haiku all you want, but fussing and wanting and desiring and demanding will all come to nothing.

One aspect of writing haiku is simple in that when something hits you, you just state what you are sensing at that moment. As Shiki instructed, one should record "the objective description of objects, and through them the stimulation of the emotions of the reader."

As to subject matter, the traditional Japanese haiku focused on nature by using seasonal words and topics. I feel that because all manmade objects are ultimately made of materials existing in nature, any topic is open to haiku use. Things we think of as unpleasant or ugly have no evaluation when used in a haiku—they just are:

nomi shirami	fleas, lice
uma no shitosuru	the horse peeing
makuramoto	near my pillow
—Bashō	

Haiku are not about exotica. They are about the everyday, so everyone can readily understand them. As to form and rules, you can't differ from the Japanese too much or else your effort won't be a haiku, but how much is not too much? I usually start with what I think is the essence of a haiku — the intense sensual moment when I identify with an external scene and lose sense of self. Since that is the essence of haiku for me, what form do I choose? I prefer to stay with Blyth's three lines of two beats, three beats, two beats; using only capitals for proper names; and as little punctuation as possible. Jane Reichhold has said that by using punctuation, in most cases the writer has copped out and hasn't distinguished the two parts of the haiku clearly enough because of their inadequate choice of words. I agree, but I do have a weakness for ellipses (" . . . ") to indicate a pause. The haiku is one moment in time with usually two images being juxtaposed. As Shiki stated so well, "through juxtaposition antitheses are harmonized."

Using Betty Drevniok's rule that a haiku should contain a comparison, a contrast, or an association is fine for beginners to learn the structure of haiku. But after a while it will become automatic, and when a moment that moves you occurs, the form for writing the haiku will come up spontaneously. Below are four examples using **comparison**, **contrast**, **association**, and **riddle**. First, a **comparison** of the wind's effect on water to its effect on summer grasses.; the two images reflect each other:

the wind
ripples across the bay
summer grasses

In the first haiku below, human consciousness is **contrasted** with that of the chicken. In the second haiku, there is **contrast** of the images in terms of size — one being small and the other large — and in terms of location — one being close and the other distant:

aki no kaze   autumn wind —
tori no miru mono   a chicken looks at something
ware ni mienu   I cannot see

  — Katō Shūson

(*Shoji*, used below, are the paper-covered doors in a traditional Japanese home.)

utsukushi ya   a thing of beauty
shoji-no ana-no   to see through the shoji's hole
ama-no-gawa   the Milky Way

  — Issa

In the haiku below, the writer has drawn an **association** between the smoke rising and the rain coming down, and both are visible in the frame of the skylight:

the skylight frames
incessant rain and
wood-stove smoke

Sometimes a haiku presents a confusion between one thing and another in the form of a **riddle**. The most common one is a flower or fruit being confused with something such as a bird or butterfly:

a red fruit
so early on the cherry tree?
no . . . a hummingbird

red pepper pods . . .
if you add wings to them
they are dragonflies

    — Bashō

Is it necessary to have or have had the experience one is
recording in a haiku? Some haijin question the validity
of "desk" haiku — haiku written from dreams, or while
musing, etc. — compared to haiku written from immediate
experience. I am open to the idea of "desk haiku," but feel
that inspiration that comes from dreams, imaginings, ideas,
and other "head" phenomena tends to feel too contrived.
For those kinds of inspirational moments I prefer to write
a longer poem. Shiki states that "if you use imaginary
pictures you will get both good and bad haiku, but the good
ones will be rare. If you use real pictures [images], it is still
difficult to get very good haiku, but it is comparatively easy
to get second-class ones."

Jane Reichhold was not against "desk haiku," such as
ones written from an idea or from simply playing around
with words. She felt that the satori moment has been over
accentuated and that moments of awareness, insight, and
inspiration don't have to be of a high spiritual nature to
produce good haiku. This opinion has been very liberating,
I think, to those haijin who feel that aiming for the satori
moment is just too ambitious. However, for me, playing
with ideas seems just too far away from the Japanese haiku
tradition to justify it being called haiku. The desk-haiku
writer tends to stay too far outside the images he or she
is writing about to get that selfless moment that unites all
nature (human, animal, earth, the universe), and that, I feel,
is the essence of haiku. Of course, all haiku are written *after*

the moment, if one wants to be exact, and Michael Dylan Welch puts it succinctly when he states, "vibrancy of the experience is more important than recency."

Now for the break — the pause after the first five or first twelve phonetic sounds in traditional Japanese haiku. As I will explain later when considering kireji (cutting words) in English, the break can be indicated by a dash or an ellipsis. The aim is to juxtapose two strong images obtained from the senses that cause your mind to take a leap and open in order to allow you to have a wider, deeper understanding of the scene you are recording. The images could indicate the what? when? and where? of the haiku moment, (object + time + place) or something eternal, something passing, and something linking the two. The answers to what? when? and where? really define the moment, and this information is present in all good haiku, I feel.

In this well-known haiku by Bashō, **what?** is the "sound of water," **when?** is when "a frog jumps in," and **where?** is at "the old pond." Alternately, the old pond could represent the **permanent element**, the frog jumping in is the **passing element** (as life passes), the sound of water is what **links** the two:

furu ike ya	old pond
kawazu tobikomu	a frog jumps in . . .
mizu no oto	the sound of water

Of course one does not have time to think what? when? where? or eternal, passing, and link at the moment when the haiku pops into your consciousness.

Can haiku rhyme? No rhyme for me. A rhyme closes the haiku and I feel the haiku should be left wide open. Rhyme also distracts with its cleverness. Harold G. Henderson, in *The Bamboo Broom*, rhymes all of his translations of the Japanese haiku, and though he tries to be as sensitive as possible, still his rhymes force the words on to the page. Henderson also adds titles, again I feel it's a move that hinders the openness of the haiku. Dorothy Britton rhymed the first and third line in her translation of haiku for Bashō's *The Narrow Road to the Deep North*, and they have a quaint Victorian ring about them, like this very ladylike translation of the poem given earlier:

> Fleas and lice did bite;
> And I'd hear the horse pass water
> Near my bed at night.

Alexey Andreyev replies to the question of whether rhyme is allowable in haiku by stating, "Correct spelling is also "unnatural," not even talking about writing from left to right which is 'unnatural' not only for left-handed people and Arabs but also for the very haiku inventors, ancient Japanese, who wrote their texts from top to bottom." He makes the point that if rhymes flow naturally for you, then put them in. Since the majority of Japanese words finish in a vowel, haiku written in Japanese will rhyme much more often than haiku written in English. I feel the same about rhyme in haiku as I do about other literary techniques such as alliteration, in that they can be too self-conscious and therefore impede spontaneity. It is true, however, that in Japanese haiku, the use of alliteration and onomatopoeic words is considered very desirable.

Of the writing process, Daisetz Suzuki says that concentration is needed before the unconscious can be tapped. By becoming the pine, as Bashō recommends, this single-pointed concentration is achieved and the haiku slips through. I believe that the very best haiku are written from this state of concentration, which is known as *samadhi* (*sammai* in Japanese), when there is no skin between you and the images you are writing about; when the archer, the bow, the arrow, and the target all become one. From this state, a deep understanding of the universe arises. Suzuki said, "Where satori flashes, there is the tapping of creative energy; where creative energy is felt, art breathes *yūgen*." *Yūgen* is a quality expressing a deep mysteriousness which I will elaborate on in a later chapter.

All very esoteric, yet the paradox about haiku is that writers use ordinary words to write about what they are experiencing or have experienced. Meanwhile something else is clear to them, something deeper, touching on the mystery of it all.

Haiku should be written in a totally relaxed, receptive way, but with some part of one's being having the intensity of a last act. A good haiku raises questions, but should not have any "reasoning" in it, e.g., haiku should never tell how "this" is happening because of "that."

For me, two things mark a good haiku. One is a sense that the haijin has found his or her own viewpoint, and secondly, that viewpoint hints of the interrelatedness of all things in the universe. Hans Hoffman, the painter, expressed such relationships this way: "Nature is always the artist's best source of inspiration, but in its spiritual, not physical sense. In nature every object exists in relationship to other things. This is what we must seek." The interconnectedness is already there; it is up to the haijin to reveal it directly and simply.

If the haijin concentrates on describing the external reality, then the true essence of the interaction between nature and human nature will come through. Bashō tried to write each haiku as though it was his last and therefore produced a greater percentage of "good" haiku than most haijin, even though he modestly denied it.

All this can only lead to the conclusion that haiku is not merely formula poetry! Because each poem is of the moment and what the moment demands, haiku cannot be written to formula, nor used for political or religious promotion — although another level of viewing, that some call "spiritual," is inevitable. A "spiritual" moment does not, however, guarantee a good haiku. Only a suitable choice of words can do that. When it comes to a final analysis, I recommend not bothering about whether the haiku is "good" or "bad," but just ask yourself, "Is this the way I want to write it?"

It always amazes me that such a small poem is fenced in with so many rules. Rules and technique can totally obscure the basis of haiku, which I feel is seeing with what Clark Strand calls the "beginner's mind," the ability to see (or use the other senses) without an overlay of concepts and opinions. Bashō instructed, "learn the rules and then forget them."

Jane Reichhold actually listed sixty-five rules for writing haiku; some of these rules have come, and some have gone, and some have been around a long time. Luckily she adds, "no one really knows how to write a haiku," and so she too makes this recommendation: "try strict rules, try breaking the rules . . . but keep trying." Mechanical rules are not enough; they are, in my opinion, overruled every time by the freshness of the images.

You can't be taught how to write haiku, although the way of haiku can be roughly pointed out. It is only when haijin have "turned around" deep inside that haiku-writing becomes real and not just a form to be applied.

R. H. Blyth felt the most satisfactory haiku has a "twist" at the end that shocks the readers awake or surprises them with "something one knew all the time, but did not know one knew":

> at the height
> of the argument — the old couple
> pour each other tea.
> —George Swede

> the heron
> pecks at its reflection
> shallow water

"Shallow" here is not used as a negative term. It implies that things are in front of the eye, things are not concealed.

Although one cannot really teach anyone else to write haiku, there do seem to be some qualities in life that might be fertile ground for haiku writing. Blyth listed "selflessness, loneliness, grateful acceptance, humor, wordlessness, non-intellectuality, freedom, courage, contradictoriness, non-morality, simplicity, love, and materiality," as states of mind that might be useful to encourage the haiku into existence.

Tom Clausen, on his website *A Haiku Way of Life*, gives a parallel list: "Faith, sharing, discipline, concision, solitude, humility, awareness, ritual, creativity, centering, truthfulness, curiosity, and patience." Either Blyth's or Clausen's list would be a fine aspiration for any human life and confirms my feeling that although anyone can produce at least one good haiku (I have proof of that from the many workshops I have given), on the whole it is the state of being of the writer that allows a steady flow of fairly good haiku, and, perhaps, more than the average number of hair-tingling ones, to appear.

My list of qualities often present in a good haiku writer might include clarity of perception, awareness, simplicity, openness, and absence of any rigid ethical standards. Haiku are not judgmental. I would add that a childlike way of viewing the world is essential.

Now for those kigo (seasonal words) and the kireji (punctuation) that will help you in your writing of haiku.

KIGO (SEASONAL WORDS) AND KIDAI (SEASONAL TOPICS)

HAIKU ARE TRADITIONALLY ABOUT THE SEASONS AND
usually include a *kigo* — a word or phrase indicating the
season about which the haiku is being written:

ochiba ochi	*falling leaves fall*
kasanarite ame	*and pile up; the rain*
ame wo utsu	*strikes the rain . . .*
—Gyōdai	

Ochiba — falling leaves — is the kigo here, indicating that
the haiku was written about autumn.

Are the Japanese more seasonally conscious than people of
other countries, I wonder? In Japan it is possible to buy *saijiki* —
books of seasonal words — which are often from five to six
hundred pages long. These seasonal words have been used
for hundreds of years by haijin in order to indicate at what
time of year the haiku is about. By using the saijiki, a suitable
kigo can be pre-selected — a good thing to do before going to
a *renga* (linked verse) meeting. So much for spontaneity!

The Japanese often use a single image, modifying it to
refer to various seasons; for example, *hasu* (lotus) usually
indicates midsummer, but if it is modified, it can mean
other seasons. *Maki-hasu* (curling lotus) would indicate
early summer; *yari-hasu* (broken lotus) would point to
autumn; and *kare-hasu* (withered lotus) would indicate the
haiku was written about winter. *Kidai* (broad images), in
this case *hasu* (lotus), are in this way subdivided within the

saijiki. Sometimes kigo, the more specific image, such as "cherry blossom," rather than "flower," can indicate slightly different times of the year also; for example, the cherry blossoms open earlier in Okinawa, and days or even weeks later, they open in northern Japan, as the cherry blossom wave moves northwards. By the way, Japanese understand that when the word for flower (*hana*) is used on its own, it can only mean the cherry blossom!

The Japanese have made the seasons the predominant theme for haiku. Haiku are often written in a natural setting and the moment is, of course, defined by the season. The season, one could say, anchors the haiku. In Japan, New Year's Day, the most important holiday of the year, is counted as a season in its own right. Nowadays Japanese kigo can also include Christmas, Easter, April Fool's Day, Valentine's Day, and other Western imports. When using kigo for haiku in English, it is preferred that they not refer to things so local that they have no significance outside the area, otherwise the haiku cannot be widely shared. The traditional Japanese kigo tie the haiku within the long and comparatively homogeneous Japanese cultural history.

Because the haiku is a very compressed poetic form, the use of a seasonal word is handy, since in a few phonetic sounds the Japanese can understand immediately what season is being written about. For example:

kaidō ni   along the highway
shōji o shimete   sliding doors close
kami hitoe   one paper away

　　—Yamaguchi Tazuo

Shōji is the seasonal word indicating, in this case, a cool season or time of day when the doors would be closed. Every Japanese knows that shōji are sliding doors made of paper stretched on a wooden frame, and that shōji, though frail, mark off *uchi* from *soto* — the inner world of the family from the outside world of "others." The sound of shōji closing would have often been a lonely one for travelers, since it excluded them from the inner life of the village they were traveling through. All this information in just three syllables!

Robert Hass expresses this idea of the haiku as compression in this way: "It compresses the experiences of cyclical time, and the all-time-no-time of Zen in seventeen syllables. [sic] The *kigo* is the focus of this compression."

Clark Strand feels haiku make nature a spiritual path. Certainly using a moment from the natural cycle can allow the haiku, when it is read, to reach out to the ends of the universe, but then so can the image of a tin can in the gutter. Some modern haijin exclude the kigo in the writing of haiku. They feel that just focusing deeply on the subject alone, manmade or natural, will inevitably, at some level, pull you into an awareness of the seasons and the ephemeralness of all things. All things that come into being must pass away, but nowadays, when people no longer even know the source of their food or water supply, it is even more important to use images directly from the natural cycle to remind people that they are intimately interrelated to the world outside themselves. As Patricia Donegan says, writing haiku is "a deep way to practice deep ecology."

Here is a list of a few seasonal words characteristic of classical Japanese haiku:

spring: frogs, cherry blossom, plum blossom, iris, butterfly, skylarks, swallows

summer: water lilies, rain, peonies, river, firefly, waterfall, mountain climbing, cicadas

autumn: dogs, geese, moon viewing, a deer crying, crows, pampas grass, red/yellow leaves, chrysanthemums, peaches, persimmon, grapes

winter: layers of quilted clothes, peonies, bells ringing, snow viewing, fallen leaves

KIREJI (CUTTING WORDS)

THERE IS NO PUNCTUATION IN TRADITIONAL JAPANESE haiku. The pause that defines the two complementary or contrasting images is marked by a kireji, or cutting word. These "cutting" words act as caesuras, adding depth to the haiku by heightening its emotional impact. The pause a kireji allows adds a greater significance to the haiku, and it is within this gap that the reader's imagination can get going. Kireji are usually inserted after the 5th or 12th phonetic sound in traditional 17-phonetic-sound haiku, breaking them into 5, 12 or 12, 5 phonetic sounds.

Because we have no equivalent to a kireji in English, when translating haiku written in Japanese or when writing them in English, we have to indicate the pause or accentuate a certain word in other ways. For example, the line end — if the haiku is written in three lines — can indicate the pause, or, if the position of the pause is not obvious, it can be accentuated by a dash or an ellipsis. I favor ellipses because they indicate a trailing off into silence. There is usually only one pause in a haiku, for if more are used, the brief poem would be broken up too much, and the contrast of the two images would be unclear.

I'll list a few of the eighteen kireji used in traditional Japanese haiku here and suggest equivalents that can be used for the same purpose when writing haiku in English.

Kana is equivalent in English to "ah!" "alas!" or a deep sigh, and is often indicated in English by using an ellipsis or an exclamation mark. Kana usually occurs at the end of a haiku when writers want to tell you that although they haven't spelled out the emotions they are feeling as they write, nevertheless they are strong. Here an exclamation point has been used in the English version:

> tsurigane ni
> tomarite nemuru
> kocho kana
>
> — Buson

> on the hanging bell
> stopping while asleep
> a butterfly!

Keri accentuates the importance of the verb. In English haiku, an ellipsis is often used if necessary. Here the verb "*some*" ("dyeing") is accentuated by keri:

> tsuki no yuki
> ao-ao yami o
> some ni keri
>
> — Kawabata Bōsha

> snow under the moon
> so blue, dyeing the darkness
> with its blue

Here keri accentuates the verb "*tomari*" (settles):

> kare eda ni
> karasu no tomari keri
> aki no kure
>
> — Bashō

> on a withered branch
> a crow settles . . .
> autumn twilight

Ka — our question mark is the equivalent:

> aogaeru
> onore no penki
> nuritate ka
>
> — Akutagawa Ryūnosuke

> green frog
> have you also been
> freshly painted?

Yara is used after a rhetorical question that expects no reply; for example, "I wonder":

tombo-tsuri	my dragon-fly hunter
kyō wa doko made	where has he wandered today
itta yara	I wonder?

—Chiyo-ni

Ya is sometimes added to a noun to convert the noun from an immediate object into one of deeper symbolism; it's a way to say, "Consider what has just been written." A "!" or sometimes "Oh!" is used in translation:

mi ni shimu ya	a penetrating chill!
naki tsuma no kushi wo	the comb of my long dead wife
neya ni fumu	underfoot in the bedroom

—Buson

In this second example, a dash has been substituted in the English version:

mijikayo ya	night grows short —
asai ni kaki no	scooping up a persimmon flower
hana o kumu	from shallow water

—Buson

Although some haiku writers wouldn't agree with her, Jane Reichhold suggests that "when a strong stop is needed, a colon could be used. A pause could be shown by using a semicolon, and something left unsaid by an ellipsis. When the image is accentuated, either directly by using additional words to describe it, or by the use of a parallel image, a long dash can be used":

wet beach sand —
a sandpiper's song
of footprints

— Michael Dylan Welch

David Cobb points out that the kireji at the end of the haiku
stimulates a mood, and I agree. Haiku should be read at
least twice — once to grasp the scene presented, and once to
let the image really sink in and so play with the responding
internal vibrations. It is good to reread the haiku having
shifted one's emotional state somewhat. Cobb also reminds
us that in the writing of Japanese haiku, the kireji is often
omitted if the sense obviously indicates a hiatus. This is,
of course, very much the way we write haiku in English,
as I said, relying on the line break to present a hiatus. In
Japanese, since the haiku is often written in one long line,
there are no line breaks, so the kireji is important; "cutting
up the worm" is how it is described. Some Japanese haijin
feel that the presence of kireji in a haiku is even more
important than sticking to the 5, 7, 5 phonetic sound rule.

THOSE JAPANESE SENSITIVITIES

WHILE THE CHOOSING OF A SEASONAL WORD OR EVEN
learning how to indicate pauses is comparatively easy for
the non-Japanese writer of haiku, many Japanese feel that
foreigners, when reading translations of Japanese haiku,
can't possibly understand references to Chinese or Japanese
historical places and figures. Even more importantly,
foreigners can't possibly appreciate the particularly
Japanese-sensitive qualities, such as *wabi, sabi,* and *makoto,*
that go toward making a fine haiku.

Daisetz Suzuki says that "to understand the spirit of Zen
along with haiku, a thorough acquaintance with Japanese
psychology and surroundings is essential." Maybe that
is true for some Japanese haiku, but that statement does
contain a hint of cultural chauvinism. It may indeed
be true that for understanding the world, the sensing/
intellectual approach works better for non-Japanese than
the feeling/intuiting way of the Japanese, but that doesn't
mean the latter is inaccessible to us. When Suzuki states
that "haiku is a poetic form possible only for the Japanese
mind and the Japanese language, to the development
of which Zen has contributed its respectable quota," he
does his country a disservice. Haiku does what all poetry
does — intensifies experience — and that is surely not
the prerogative of any one nation. Is it possible that the
understanding of the essence of wabi and sabi occupy a
particular gene in Japanese people that the non-Japanese
don't have?

Uchida Sonō supports Suzuki's view, however, in that he

feels that the Japanese are more suited to the writing of haiku than non-Japanese since they view "man as part of the natural world and [man] should live in harmony with it"; whereas, the Western way of thinking, "in which man is regarded as being independent of, and perhaps superior to, the rest of nature," is definitely not conducive to the writing of haiku. This may have been true to a certain extent at one time, but anyone observing Japan's present-day economic ventures, garbage in the countryside, pollution in the harbors, not to mention nuclear power plant disasters, can admit the distinction between East and West may have blurred somewhat in this respect. Western haijin may actually be as skilled as their Japanese counterparts when it comes to their ability to respect their interdependence with the natural world and their ability to fuse with their subjects and produce a good haiku:

> *fuyu-kawa niin*　　　　the winter river
> *shinbun zenshia*　　　　complete newspaper,
> *tsukari uku*　　　　soaked through, floats
> 　　—Yamaguchi Seishi

As Jim Kacian points out, "haiku has moved well beyond the limitations it might once have had as being considered strictly a Japanese form, and has become indeed, the most practiced poetic form around the world, being written now in over fifty languages."

Let's take a closer look at some of those "nontransferable" qualities that Daisetz Suzuki set so much store by.

WABI

Wabi originally meant the misery of having to live alone in nature, away from society. Now it still means lonely, not in the rejected sense, but more in the sense of Suzuki's "haiku is loneliness itself," and he quotes Bashō as the finest example of this. "Wabi is the aesthetic appreciation of absolute poverty," is another Suzuki statement. By this, he doesn't mean the degradation that poverty usually brings, but that we should not be dependent on things worldly, not be in the fashionable society of the time, not be "with it" — whatever "it" is at this moment. Wabi respects the ordinary, the unpretentiousness of everyday life as distinct from the continual "Wow!" of show business and advertising. Wabi defines subjective elements, inner states. It is about being content within oneself, content with insufficiency. It embraces the morality of Buddhism that Suzuki defines as "free of greed, violence, anger, indolence, uneasiness, and folly."

SABI

Wabi and sabi are sometimes used in hyphenated form (by Western interior decorators!) and their definitions are often confused; even Suzuki says they are interchangeable. Sabi originally meant chill, lean, withered. Now its meaning is closer to elegant simplicity — the beautiful patina of things that have been well-used; a sort of rustic unpretentiousness; a flawed item, the flaw making it perfect, as with a broken gate or a cup with a crack in it. Sabi suggests the aura of loneliness that a common everyday thing can give rise to. Bashō accentuated the "lonely beauty" aspect of the word, the idea that all things must die, and because of this they have within them a beauty of a deeper kind. This solitary melancholy should not be judged, but just accepted, and from the acceptance comes joy. Sabi is used objectively to describe things in the "outer" world.

AWARE

The awareness that all is suffering sets one free from the angst of life on earth. *Aware* (pronounced a-wa-ray) is the sweetness and brevity of life, the pathos of an object in that its beauty lies in its fragility and ephemeralness (*mujo*). It hints at the bitter-sweetness of life and the "touchingness" of things. Aware is a nostalgic sadness that everything must pass. The concept *miyabi* is often linked with *aware*. Miyabi implies perfection both with form and color, but also implied is that this beauty is a passing one and so has a touch of sadness attached.

YŪGEN

Yūgen is an awareness of the universe that gives rise to a feeling of extreme awe. Suzuki defines yūgen as an "awareness of a spiritual rhythm, a glimpse of things eternal in the world of constant changes." Yūgen is the beauty of the mystery and impenetrability of the universe, its unknowable depths, the small in contrast to the cosmic. I feel yūgen frees us from the illusion of finiteness.

MAKOTO

Makoto is about sincerity, expressing sincere feelings. The saying, "Nothing is haiku unless it is sincere," by Uejima

Onitsura, suggests the childlike quality of a pure heart that can see things clearly.

SHIBUI

Quiet, soberly restrained, quietly elegant, beyond style or fashion — these qualities suggest *shibui*. The Japanese use the persimmon to personify this stringent quality where things are subtly suggested in a simple, refined way.

HON-I

Hon-i is the ability to see things in unsophisticated ways, ways that are not masked by deceit, phoniness, calculation, or discrimination. It suggests bringing something down to its essence, as in "to be what it is."

KARUMI

Bashō recommended that, above all, haiku should have the quality of *karumi* (lightness). By this he did not mean that the haiku should be flippant, but that whatever was presented — a dead dog, a rose, urine, prostitutes, or cherry blossoms — should be presented in a disinterested way, or as the Buddhists would say, with nonattachment. Everything — tasteful or distasteful — is interesting and should be looked at as subject matter, ordinary subjects written about in a simple way. As John Blofeld, the Buddhist scholar, said, "loss, decay and death are just as natural as gain, growth and life."

In a blurring of identity, Japanese haijin seem to anthropomorphize more than seems acceptable among non-Japanese, who tend to shy away from sparrows that play and horses that stop to view the cherry blossoms. When anthropomorphism is used in English haiku-writing, perhaps it is hard for it not to sound cute and affected; whereas to the Japanese, the anthropomorphism sounds perfectly natural and a sign that good empathy between writer and subject has happened:

> kaitsuburi   the grebe
> sabishiku nareba   becoming lonely
> kuguri-keri   dives into the water
>
> — Hino Sōjō

HAIKU AND EMOTION

BUT WHAT ABOUT EMOTION ITSELF? HAIKU DO NOT actually mention emotions directly in spite of them being about moments of heightened emotion.

If there is too much emotion in a haiku, there is too much of you and not enough absorption with the subject—that absorption, perhaps, being the essence of haiku. You will find, however, that if you describe the subject clearly enough, the emotion you are feeling will come through clearly. You are presenting the trigger for the emotion, rather than the actual emotion itself. Your trigger, if it is strong enough, will give rise to the emotion when the haiku is read. We don't need weeping and wailing to show how deeply the moment has touched us—no "How sad!" "How terrible!" "How evil!" "How wonderful!" Take Bashō's "crow on the bare branch":

kare eda ni	on a withered branch
karasu no tomari keri	a crow settles
aki no kure	autumn twilight

Does Bashō say how sad he is, sad that the year is passing, that the leaves are falling, that all must pass? No! He merely tells you that it is evening, the season is autumn, and one very black crow is on a bare branch. What could be more melancholy? This pathos and melancholy in nature was the essence of Bashō's best haiku.

Winona Baker, a fine Canadian haiku writer, stated that when writing haiku, "no explanations, moralizing or judgments are made." Clark Strand puts it so beautifully when he states that a haiku comes "from the place where objective description overlaps the heart."

T'ai Wei, an eleventh-century Chinese poet, captures the idea this way: "Poetry presents the thing in order to convey the feeling. It should be precise about the thing and reticent about the feeling, for as soon as the mind responds and connects with the thing, the feeling shows in the words; this is how poetry enters deeply into us." In other words, stay with "the thing," and the emotion will become clear.

WHAT TO LEAVE OUT

THE HAIKU MOMENT IS SO INTENSE AND RICH IN ITS
reverberations that the writer cannot possibly put all he or
she wants to say about it into three short lines. As David
Quammen so aptly said about poetry in general, "a good
poem is a one-eyed glimpse of a bird in flight. Poetry's special
grace and special challenge is compaction — the compaction
of language and meaning and time." And when you only
have three lines and want to express a universe of amazement,
compaction is an especially important tool. A haiku, while
using a limited number of words, outlines in the strongest
way possible what the writer has just sensed. These words in
the haiku therefore need to be carefully chosen. They should
not come between the reader and the true experience the
writer has just had; they should facilitate the passage. In the
following excellent haiku, the words present no barrier:

> a dry oblong
> where the car was parked
> at the cemetery
> —Winona Baker

Non-essential words tend to push the haijin's point of view
too much, provide too much information, and make the haiku
less open to allowing the reader to play his or her role. The
elusiveness of a haiku can draw readers in, but if too few words
are used or it is too enigmatic, readers will be puzzled. People
don't accentuate enough that writing haiku is a social activity;
whatever you have experienced, you want to communicate.
After all, haiku originated from renga, those linked verses that
involve at least two poets, often three or more. The first

seventeen phonetic syllables of a renga, which eventually split off and became what we know as haiku, are saying, "Well, we are all gathered here on this fine fall day, so let's mark the days growing shorter," — some type of greeting that sets the time and the mood of the group poetry session. In Bashō's day, the joy of writing renga was the interaction between the teacher and fellow poets, so communication was imperative. The aim is to have a haiku to which nothing needs to be added or taken away in order to allow the reader the joy of "getting" what the haijin is saying, a haiku that gives readers room to expand the haiku according to their own individual reading of it.

There are no articles in Japanese, so many haijin do the same in English, but this then sounds like the English of a beginning student learning the language — very stilted and choppy. Often the first image of the haiku doesn't have an article attached, whereas the phrase containing the contrasting or complementary image and the line linking the two images will use the article. That is, the longer part of the haiku has the article included so it sounds more like a complete statement. Here "spring memorial" is the subject; "dampness, etc." is the complementing addition and so has "the" added:

> spring memorial
> the dampness
> in a handful of soil
> > —Alice Frampton

There is no room for metaphors and similes in haiku. You

are spontaneously describing a scene and have no time to compare it to something else by saying, "it was like a . . ." I complain about Diane Ackerman's profuse use of metaphor in a poem I wrote: "On Reading Diane Ackerman." These lines could well apply to the writing of haiku:

> she continually
> says "this" is like "that"
> and why she doesn't say
> how "this" is like "this."
> Bashō could show her . . .

The likeness is implied in the objects you have chosen to juxtapose. For example, in Bashō's famous poem of the crow settling on the branch at twilight, one could use the simile "the crow settling on the branch is like twilight settling on the day," but one doesn't need to say all that, because it is implied in Bashō's intuitive grasp of the moment. With a metaphor or simile, the likeness is firmly stated. This is not the way of haiku, where the similarity must not be noted in an outspoken way. Having said that, however, I should state that most good haiku have a hidden metaphor.

Some poets mistakenly think that "I" shouldn't be used in haiku since the writer is the assumed watcher; therefore it is unnecessary to mention who is taking part in the action. This is not correct, for "I" can be used just as objectively as a chair or any other subject, as in this haiku by Shiki (for the Japanese *romaji* version of this haiku, see the later reference to Shiki):

> looking back
> the man I greeted just now —
> only the mist

Here are other favorites of mine in which the word "I" is essential to be included:

nami ni atokata
mo nashi onna to
oyogishi ga
　—Yamaguchi Seishi

in the waves no trace
even though I once swam here
with a woman

ari korosu
ware o sannin no ko
ni mirarenu
　—Katō Shūson

I kill an ant
then see my three children
have been watching

mienu meno
hō-no megane-no
tama mo fuku
　—Hino Sōjō

it's sight lost
yet for that eye-glass
I also polish

Haiku is poetry of the ordinary for ordinary people. (Tanka, on the other hand, were historically written mostly by nobility.) Do not use unusual language to write haiku — the more ordinary the better — and compound words overload the haiku. I think it was possibly Blyth who said, "Haiku is like pointing a finger to the moon. If the finger is covered in rings, you will never look at the moon, you will be transfixed by the rings." In haiku writing, take off those rings and let's see the moon. Haiku is simply what is happening in this place at this moment, so make the moment as clear as you can. As Blyth stated, "the immediate life experience is the essence."

Kenneth Yasuda says this nicely, "A haiku poet does not give us meaning, he gives us objects that have meaning; he does not describe, he presents."

As to analysis of and explanations for haiku, I firmly agree with Michael Dylan Welch when he says that "any haiku that needs footnotes isn't doing its job." Henderson adds, "Haiku were not written to be weighed down with commentary." "The instant you speak about a thing you miss the mark," is an appropriate Zen saying.

Finally, don't try to be brilliant or innovative. In fact, stop trying. The desire to be thought witty or sensitive will come between the poet and his or her insight. Henderson again, "Really great haiku suggest so much that more words would lessen their meaning." Ueda adds, "With only slight exaggeration it might be said that the haiku poet completes only half of his poem, leaving the other half to be supplied in the reader's imagination." To this, Bashō states, "showing seventy to eighty percent of a subject is good, but people never tire of reading haiku that only show fifty to sixty percent."

Haiku do not express ideas; the writer does not tell what has been going on in his or her mind. Rather, the writer uses strong images to reflect the emotion the haijin had at the moment of writing. That is why haiku is said to be the poetry of nouns. Adjectives and adverbs are neglected as they expand the haiku too much; they also tend to be judgmental (e.g., ugly, beautiful). Adjectives don't leave the readers space to do their work. It is up to the strong nouns to outline the image and allow the reader to sense the emotions behind the haiku. As Tom Hoover says, "There is no comment; the images are simply thrown out to give the mind a starting point."

Once I went out to view Christmas lights with a small child. The father pointed out where the child should look as he drove. "Left, right, left, right." he said. The child, overwhelmed by the lights, called out "Weft, light, weft, light!" We also call out in amazement when we, as haijin, receive a haiku, but the haiku moment we record should be understandable to others.

A haiku is not a neurotic, self-indulgent poem. It is a moment that should be able to be shared, and so the haiku must not be so personal or so intellectual that its subject cannot be understood by most readers. In fact, haiku should never be a display of intellectual brilliance. I can't accentuate enough that haiku are poems of the five senses. When it comes to sharing, certainly some of the references in Japanese haiku may have been to images in Chinese literature that only scholars might know about, but these references were understood in the homogeneous, literate haiku circles of the time when they were written. An example is the idea of Tao — the "spiritual way" — often found in Japanese haiku written as *kanji* (Chinese symbol), for "road."

Images reflect a deep intuition and while the intuition cannot be transferred to others, the images can. The reader must be able to catch the intuition behind the images, otherwise the images are just items for intellectual analysis and the haiku is lost. Trite images produce trite haiku.

EDITING HAIKU

Yes, it's true. Bashō did not write the first line of his famous frog poem immediately, but considered the scene and added it later. But, being Bashō, he could.

I think that for most of us, editing removes us from the "here and now" of the scene to moments later when the intensity has passed. Editing then becomes a matter of ego, making sure you have correct words that will be considered sound, if not perfect. A child, as my friend's son quoted in the previous chapter, just lets words tumble out. That is direct seeing. Editing, I feel, is hair-splitting and takes away from the immediate impact of the image/s that inspired the haiku. Don't forget Bashō was also the one who advised that haiku be written as swiftly as "a woodcutter fells a tree, or a swordsman leaps at a dangerous enemy." In either case, stopping to look for an eraser would be foolhardy if not downright dangerous. I should say that not everyone agrees with me about this. Some consider "not editing" just as much an act of ego, and editing could be considered an act of humility in that it seeks clarity in order that the reader won't misread the haiku. I feel that the reader will take what they want from the haiku, and a writer can never guarantee a perfect match between his or her intention and the reader's interpretation.

Haiku is about a unique moment. How can it be unique when a week later you are still switching words and lines? Haiku are unselfconscious — the self is nowhere to be found, so how can editing take place? Nowadays haijin are somewhat relaxed about editing, however, and feel that if the original intensity can be maintained, editing is fine. After all, if the reader can better share the emotion that produced the haiku, isn't that what the writer wants? Still, Bashō commands "Let there not be a hair's breadth separating your mind from what you write. Quickly say what is in your mind; never hesitate a moment."

I am profligate with my haiku, and if they don't resonate later, I throw them out. While living in Japan, I remember how upset I was when a student of mine told me how he prepared his haiku before going to a so-called spontaneous contest. I like to keep my illusion that spontaneity is the essence of haiku.

All that being said, at our annual haiku gathering that I hosted for many years on the island of Gabriola, in British Columbia, where I live, the haiku we wrote while taking the *ginko* (inspirational walk) would later be presented anonymously to the group. The gentle, sensitive haijin present proceeded to shred them into tatters. Well, not really. But we did want to grasp the moment that the haijin had recorded, and we did want to help that record be as clear and as concise as possible so that the haiku allowed us, on reading it, to extrapolate to the emotions, ideas, and intuitions to which it could give rise, but which it didn't express directly. These annual critiquing sessions never failed to draw me more deeply into aspects of haiku I hadn't penetrated before.

HAIKU? SENRYŪ?

THE DEBATE AS TO WHETHER A VERSE IS A HAIKU OR *senryū* is much more important outside of Japan. In Japan, if you belong to a senryū group, your poem is considered a *senryū*. Yet if you belong to a haiku group, the very same poem might be considered a haiku.

You may find the word senryū in your reading about haiku, and it will probably be mentioned in a discussion about whether a certain haiku is really a haiku or whether it is a senryū. People seem to waste a lot of time trying to sort out these two forms of three-lined verse:

> usagi mo
> kata mimi taruru
> taisho kana

> even the rabbit
> has one ear drooping
> the dog days of summer!

—Akutagawa Ryūnosuke

Haiku? Senryū? One could be very black and white and say senryū use sardonic wit or bitter irony to poke fun at the human condition; whereas haiku, by speaking indirectly of human nature by the use of natural images, show compassion toward the state of humanity.

Senryū are named after Karai Hachiemon, whose pen name was Senryū and who was a collector of witty haiku from the renga they occurred in. Here is a senryū by Alan Pizzarelli that well defines the human condition:

bzzZ
  slaP
bzzZ

Pizzarelli defines senryū as "a short poetic form which focuses on people: men, women, husbands, wives, children, relatives and other relations. It portrays the characteristics of human beings and psychology of the human mind." This definition allows for the fact that not all senryū are witty, for some dwell on the misfortunes, hardships, and woes of humanity.

Michael Dylan Welch offers a very fine analysis of this debate about what is a senryū and what is not. Welch defines senryū as similar to haiku except that they tend to be more satirical or ironic in tone and do not need to include a seasonal word or have a two-part structure. Nonetheless, some senryū include these elements and are still considered to be senryū.

In this wonderful haiku? senryū? by LeRoy Gorman, "manger" could be a seasonal word, but use of the word "cowboy" would rather lean this haiku toward senryū. Yet the profundity of searching for Jesus at a Western-style Christmas event speaks volumes:

to finish the manger
I search for Jesus
and settle for a cowboy doll

Alexey Andreyev makes the interesting distinction that "humor in senryū may be called 'destructive': it points out some absurd, negative phenomena . . . leads to an ironic,

even sarcastic smirk. On the other hand, humor in haiku
. . . is close to 'zero-emotion' level; it's an invisible smile
of a sage who sees some hidden connection between
things . . . a gentle, maybe a bit sad, smile."

When it comes to the haiku /senryū debate, Blyth helps
by pointing out that "senryū touch all our most sensitive
spots and tell us the very thing we do not wish to know." I
find Blyth's quote, "the secret of life consists in being always
and never serious," very relevant here. Further, Blyth says,
"The way of senryū is that of understanding all things by
laughing or smiling at them, and this means forgiving all
things, ourselves and God included":

after Thanksgiving
the remaining turkey
gobbles
—Alice Frampton

two men
in deep conversation . . .
a pile of manure

David Cobb wrote a brilliant essay on the subject: "Humour
in Haiku." It appeared in *Haijinx* in the summer 2001 issue
[http://www.haijinx.com/I-2/cobb/h2.html]. Himself no
mean haijin, here is one of his *senryū*:

Convent — on the line
a nun's washed black stockings
slap across my face

And let's finish this debate with a quote from Ōnishi Tasuyō on the subject: "The only distinction that can be made between haiku and senryū is by the author's name."

For more information about this topic, please consult this website: [http://graceguts.com/essays/everything-you-always-wanted-to-know-about-haiku-and-senryu-but-were-too-busy-writing-to-ask]

HAIBUN

A MIXTURE OF PROSE AND HAIKU IS CALLED A *HAIBUN*.
When it describes a journey, it is called a *kikōbun* (travel
journal). *The Narrow Road to the Deep North*, sometimes
translated as *Narrow Road to the Interior*, is Bashō's most
famous *kikōbun*, recording his travels.

The haibun prose might have a reference to the scene that is
written about in the haiku and might not. In the latter case,
the mood of the haiku will at least reflect the writer's mood
at that stage of his journey.

As usual, I naively expected haijin to be spontaneous, so I
was a little disturbed to find that haibun are edited when
the traveler has returned home. Bashō liked to give the
impression that he was an impoverished, lonely monk
dealing with the hardships of life and the primitiveness of
traveling at that time. In reality, he often had a companion
with him and sometimes stayed at the homes of wealthy
patrons. So much for illusions!

If you keep a diary, you are well on the way to writing
haibun. Just insert haiku at spots where you are feeling
intensely about a matter; remember to stay with the nouns,
and let them reflect your mood.

Here is a section of a haibun written by that fine poet
Winona Baker. It is from the book *Tidepools*:

HAIKU WEEKENDS ON GABRIOLA

To attend the annual Gabriola haiku weekend I go to the ferry
dock in downtown Nanaimo.

> once a hunter stood
> by this sea and sang —
> calling the whale

When I'm aboard the ferry I like to go on deck to enjoy the
scenery and stretch my legs. Soon we approach the island.

> postcard-blue ocean —
> by Gabriola's grey cliffs
> an orca leaps

After disembarking, it's a pleasant drive to Eli and Naomi
Wakan's home near Drumberg Park. I grew up on farms and slow
down going past the ones we see along the way.

> heady odours
> from a manure pile —
> a cock pheasant cries

Part of the first day's program is walking to Drumberg Park on a
road that ends at the sea. We're asked to write at least two haiku
on our stroll. They will be critiqued later in the day. When I arrive
at Drumberg Bay, I wade in.

> beneath water
> these stones seem
> to be breathing

HAIGA

HAIGA ARE THE SMALL SPONTANEOUS PICTURES THAT
accompany haiku. Haiga are not detailed. They are quick
sketches, but somehow such a sketch captures the vitality
and depth of a scene much better than many more labored
paintings.

Leon Zolbrod states, "the visual and literary imagination
are intimately related to a pair of the most primitive and
universal of human activities, 'babble' and 'doodle.'"
About haiga, he adds, "Poet and artist alike endeavored to
eliminate every superfluous element and to attain an austere
beauty akin to that of abstract art or to the stylized patterns
of movement in the dance element (shimai) of the Noh
drama." Zolbrod saw in haiga the influence of the purity
and simplicity of Shinto, along with the religious discipline
of Zen. He pointed out that the essence of Japanese design
is found in "the tendency to abbreviate and reduce formal
elements to the utmost degree."

Like haiku, haiga tend to be of simple things — a willow
tree, a broken fence, a heron. The line of the drawing is
flowing, and the coloring, if any, is sparse. Often haiga have
a whimsical touch, even when the haiga is of something sad.
For example, in Buson's illustration of the parting scene in
Bashō's book *The Narrow Road to the Deep North*, one or
two of the folk bidding him farewell are smiling a little.

Watanabe Kazan says of haiga, "The essence of this art is
just to sketch, to represent everything in a catchy way, and
to draw as roughly as possible. If you were to compare this

to people, someone who is wise, prudent and eloquent in practical affairs would be bad. Someone who is awkward in practical affairs and untutored would be regarded as artistic. This combination should be kept in mind."

Haiga's classical period was from the seventeenth through the nineteenth centuries, but they are still being done today. Of course, with computer programs offering ease with graphics, photo-haiga are becoming increasingly popular.

empty bus stop -
one old crow looks
at another

c.macrury

READING HAIKU

Haiku require a skilled writer and also a skilled
reader, for the reader must, in a way, become the writer. Some
haijin, when reading to an audience, read their haiku at least
twice — once to register the scene and a second time to allow
its absorption and re-creation by the listener. Likewise, when
you are reading, read the haiku again and again until you
have the image, if not the words, in your heart. Then you can
enter the scene and be engulfed by the smells, stimulated by
the texture, melted by the colors, blended into the sounds,
and fed by the tastes. Once there is no separation between the
scene and you, you are ready to let the image drift outwards
and explore its other levels. The more you read haiku this
way, the better haijin you will become.

I don't want to get caught in Daisetz Suzuki's warning that
one has to be a Zen initiate in order to understand haiku.
That is a strange kind of elitism for a form of poetry that is
actually easily available to all who step aside from their ego,
cut the intellect, and let the haiku in. Moreover, we should
remember that if we have the Zen-moment as the essence of
the haiku constantly in mind, we might miss the personal
level of the individual haijin and leap at once to profundities
without enjoying the personal images chosen on the way.

For me, a good haiku produces a sigh, an immediate sigh.
The other levels of understanding that the haiku offers —
"overtones" as Henderson calls them — may also be immediate,
or may come later. A good haiku? For me, it should raise feelings
in the reader, even though it doesn't express them directly. By
experiencing the haiku, the reader is not only put in touch with

the haijin's feelings behind the haiku, but these feelings also reverberate with the reader's own feelings. A good haiku must not just raise immediate feelings in the reader; further, deeper emotions should also resonate. It's as if by capturing the poet's moment — a part — the poet has also captured a universal truth — the whole — that reverberates with the reader.

Kaneko Tōta said, "Good haiku is everybody's haiku, but the starting point is the Self." A bad haiku? A bad haiku is one that leaves the reader wondering what is going on and what it could possibly mean. A bad haiku describes only the poet's moment and does not draw the reader in deeper.

Some people complain that reading haiku is boring, little more than a monotony of unimaginative and repetitive nature images. They argue that haiku should be more relevant, and while I am sometimes conscious of this viewpoint in myself, any good haiku journal will dispel this notion by the startling freshness of the haiku it publishes.

Many things are unstated in a haiku. As Tadao Ichiki said, "ellipsis is an important element of haiku," and it is up to the reader to sense what is in the gaps, to expand and extemporize on what is offered to his or her own satisfaction.

As said earlier, haiku are not meant to be analyzed, though they often are. A haiku is to be experienced and enjoyed, not investigated. Sam Hamill has the last word on this, "the meaning, the authentic experience of the poem, lies only within ourselves. And begins with the quality of our listening."

THE HISTORY OF HAIKU

JAPANESE POETRY, UNLIKE OCCIDENTAL, DOES NOT
consist of heroic epics or lengthy legends. The intensity
craved by the early Japanese writers came to be expressed in
a *waka* or tanka — the later name for the waka — a favorite
poetry form of the Japanese Imperial Court existing from the
eighth through the twelfth centuries. Waka consisted of 5, 7,
5, 7, 7 phonetic sounds and was thought to have developed
from early prayers and incantations to the gods.

Renga, linked waka, developed as a way of producing
poetry as a group. Renga was a very popular form of poetry
by the end of the sixteenth century. Comic renga, which
was much like a poetry game, belonged to the samurai
and peasant class, and there was a serious form used by
the nobility. At a renga gathering, one poet wrote the first
words — of 5, 7, 5 phonetic sounds respectively — which
usually had a nature theme. Another poet followed these
three with the next two sets of 7 and 7 phonetic sounds.
Then a third poet, or the first poet again, continued with
another set of 5, 7, 5 phonetic sounds, and so it went on,
usually until at least thirty-six *kasen* (sections or verses)
had been linked. But there were often more; renga's
classical form had one hundred verses, and renga of one
thousand verses have been recorded! The first set of three,
the *hokku*, the starting verse, set the tone for the renga by
concerning itself with the time and place of the writing.

Of course rules and regulations grew up around the writing
of renga — the seasons had to change as the renga proceeded,
traditional images had to be introduced, there could be no story

line, etc. Discourses were written on how the verses should be linked. Eventually, poets became impatient with the elaborate set of rules that had developed to govern renga writing, and they started to split off the first three groups of words and write them as poems in their own right, the hokku. The writing of hokku became very popular in the Edo period (1694–1867) and was much taken up by the rising merchant classes.

Another reason for the hokku splitting off from the renga was that since it set the stage for the renga, usually the most important poet at the gathering was given the honor of writing it. Poets started to prepare hokku ahead of the poetry meeting just in case they should be asked to begin the renga. So hokku were already considered apart from the rest of the renga.

Bashō was a renga master — as were Buson and Issa — and he enjoyed the light-hearted form of renga, *haikai no renga* or *renku*. By Bashō's time, renga had become merely a play on words, a witty game, where poets tried to outdo one another in cleverness. Bashō took it, and particularly the hokku, to a deeper level, perhaps through his understanding of Buddhism, but also because of his inner state of development. His students concentrated on the writing of the hokku since it was the most important part of the renga. In a way, hokku was a revolt from the elegant court tradition of waka since it used everyday language. In this way, the hokku developed into the haiku we know today.

Buson and Issa carried on Bashō's revision of *haikai* — playful linked verse covering renga, hokku, and haibun—which had once more become ossified with many rules and regulations — for example, the rule that the seasonal word should be either in the first or third phrase of the hokku. The first mention of haiku was in 1663, but it was about Issa's time that the words haikai and hokku were abbreviated to haiku. A quote by Susumu, however, about the origin of the word "haiku," has Shiki popularizing it as an abbreviation of *haikai no ku* (verse of a linked poem). Again, in later years, the writing of haikai became a formula, a sterile following of rules. Just as Bashō revived haikai writing from sterility in the seventeenth century, and Buson in the eighteenth century, so Shiki came along and refreshed the writing of haiku again at the end of the nineteenth century. Haiku, by this time, had become an accepted poetic form in its own right as distinguished from the group activities of renga. Shiki modernized the haiku, opening its subject matter and demanding a clear description of the moment as in making a *shasei* (sketch) of a scene. The haiku poet Seishi carried Shiki and haiku into the twentieth century. There were many women haijin in Japan in Shiki's period, but their position can be illustrated by the fact that the magazine *Hototogisu*, founded by Shiki, opened a "Kitchen Songs" section especially for female writers! Sugita Hisajo was just such a female writer, and in the second haiku below she strikes a little blow for the cause of women:

kochi fuku ya	easterly wind
mimi arawaruru	ears appear from
unai gami	a girl's cropped hair

tabi tsugu ya	patching tabi
nora to mo nara zu	not becoming a Nora; life
kyōshi-zuma	of a teacher's wife

Although the first foreigner recorded as writing a haiku was a certain captain in Nagasaki, Hendrick Doeff, America was prepared for haiku as we know it today by the writings of Emerson, Whitman, and Thoreau. Later, Ezra Pound's definition of an image as "an intellectual and emotional complex in an instant of time" and William Carlos William's focus on "the inner reality of the object" developed fertile ground for the haiku. The strong post-World War II connection with Japan formed the conduit.

After the war, a tired and dispirited Japan could pride itself in that at least one aspect of its culture had been picked up and run away with in admiration by the Western world. Schools of haiku working by formula may have protested the apparent damage done to haiku by its adoption in the West, but even they had to eventually admit that the fresh approach of haiku writers outside Japan had produced some remarkably fine haiku.

Americans love the efficient brevity of the haiku, and its direct observation appeals to their accentuation of the scientific. During the 1950s and early '60s, the Beatniks picked up on the Zen aspects of fusion-with-the-subject haiku, and New Age writers' accentuation on creativity encouraged all comers to try their hand. Haiku became an international form of poetry.

R. H. Blyth, Harold G. Henderson, Kenneth Yasuda, William J. Higginson, and Cor van den Heuvel all played leading roles in introducing haiku to a wider audience. The latter, in his *Haiku Anthology* (1974), managed to summarize theory and practice and a return to Bashō by selecting haiku for the anthology that best represented Bashō's emphasis on the here-and-nowness of the moment and the fusion of the haijin with the images of the haiku. Of course, Blyth's monumental four-volume set, *Haiku,* set the stage for all later writings in English.

Today there are many haiku magazines, both on and offline, and many haiku societies, not only in North America, but across Europe, South Asia, and Australasia. Haiku are often written without kigo or kireji; accentuate the human aspects of the universe, rather than the seasonal ones; and break many other aspects of traditionally written haiku. Yet this may be a sign of their vitality, for in spite of the loss of traditional haiku features, one is able to read many non-Japanese haiku and find they still arrest the heart in a moment of deep awareness.

Akito Arima is quoted as saying that perhaps "haiku written by non-Japanese may come to influence the Japanese sensitivity." I'm not sure about that, but certainly Japanese writing haiku in English are not a rare sight these days, as David McMurray of the Asahi Haikuist Network reports.

Japanese still write haiku profusely; there are many schools under haiku masters that have thousands of students. Roughly reckoned, many millions of Japanese write haiku frequently, either submitting them to regular newspaper competitions — for many newspapers have a person editing a haiku column — or at haiku gatherings at places famous for their scenery. The art of renga is also making a return and Western haijin are experimenting with this linked poetry.

As to web-haiku, there seems to be an endless supply of haiku written about computers, dogs, Jewish mothers, etc. I've even seen a web page devoted to haiku written about each American bank as it fails and one devoted to haiku based on the Periodic Table. Many haijin look on these efforts with horror and consider them a terrible corruption of their chosen form of expression. You can enter any word you like in Google—Christian haiku, horse haiku, chicken haiku—and some entry will be found. Many of these columns even instruct writers, saying "it is very easy, just 3 lines of 5 syllables, 7 syllables, 5 syllables." Even though an English syllable has no bearing on Japanese phonetic sounds. Many of these web-haiku are distasteful, being based on racial generalizations.

On new forms of haiku, Dorothy Howard, a promoter of "new form" haiku, comments rather cryptically, "exploration necessarily involves hits, near hits, near misses and misses."

Alexey Andreyev is a particularly imaginative writer of "new form" haiku. Here are some minimalist pieces of his:

> granite   water   granite
>   swinging   swinging

> bell
> Army
> Salvation
> a

Haiku writing is continually shifting and redefining itself. However haiku may develop in the future, it's time now to take a look at some of the influential haijin from the past.

THE MASTERS OF HAIKU

HERE WE WILL TAKE A LOOK AT THE MASTERS OF HAIKU:
Bashō — the progenitor, the ascetic who had a meditative
approach to haiku;
Buson — the sensual artist;
Issa — the humanist who respected all life and sought its
kami (spirit);
Chiyo-ni — the best known woman haijin of classical times;
Shiki — who rebuilt the dynasty; and
Seishi — the legitimate heir to traditional haiku.

BASHŌ

Matsuo Bashō (1644–94) saw the light of day in Ueno, Iga
Prefecture. His birth name was Matsuo Kinsaku. As a young
boy he became a page and devoted friend of his *daimyō's*
(warlord's) son. Together they wrote haikai, the light-hearted
form of linked verse and the most popular form of poetry at
that time. When his friend died, Bashō wanted to renounce the
world totally. He was twenty-two at the time. He determined
to devote his life to poetry and meditate on the ephemeralness
of all things. Although Bashō did enter a monastery, he also
traveled widely. At twenty-eight he adopted the world of Zen.
From then on, he wrote his best haiku.

In 1681 he went to live in a little hut that had a bashō
(banana tree) growing next to it, and he adopted the name
Bashō. By this time he had already become a renga master
and had a group of students studying with him.

Bashō never knew the word "haiku," which hadn't been

adopted at that time. He was concerned with developing hokku, the first 5, 7, 5 phonetic syllables of renga. Bashō raised hokku from a vulgar level, which utilized puns, to a level of simplicity and purity. Bashō accentuated the images from nature and the immediacy of their choice at the moment of composition. He also developed the haibun, the travel diaries that have haiku embedded in them. As mentioned earlier, *The Narrow Road to the Deep North* was his masterpiece haibun and covered a journey of five months. It is one of the most widely read Japanese classics.

Bashō was quoted as saying, "Those who have no traveling experience along the Tokaido are quite unlikely to become good at poetry." This statement accentuates the importance of the experience of life itself in the writing of haiku.

Blyth was very impressed by Bashō's advocacy of getting into the deepest possible contact with the greatest number of things. Bashō stated that he liked the "bringing together of melancholy things with less than melancholy things." And he felt that "all who have achieved real excellence in any art possess one thing in common; that is, a mind to obey nature, to be one with nature, throughout the four seasons of the year. Whatever such a mind sees is a flower, and whatever such a mind dreams of is the moon."

Suzuki believes Bashō to be the epitome of wabi in that he traveled with one hat, one cane stick, and one cotton bag — items enough for his wandering life. He bore the travails of primitive traveling uncomplainingly. Suzuki points out that life, too, is traveling from one point to another, and that Bashō, by traveling frequently, had more opportunity to see the parallels. As I mentioned earlier, the image of Bashō as an impoverished traveler may not have been quite accurate. We hate to be disillusioned, though, so the image of the simple traveler stays with us.

In another sense, Bashō always stayed alone, for as Suzuki said, "Bashō is a poet of Eternal Aloneness."

When asked for a death poem, Bashō said, "each of my verses has been a death haiku." His last haiku is, indeed, superb:

> tabi ni yande   ill on a journey
> yume wa kareno o   my dreams through withered fields
> kakemeguru   run wandering

He wrote this death haiku when just starting on another journey to the southwestern prefectures of Japan. He only got as far as Osaka.

When asked why he became a haijin, Bashō replied, "The fact is it knows no other art than the art of writing poetry, and therefore it hangs on to it more or less blindly" (translated by Nobuyuki Yuasa).

BUSON

Tanaguchi Buson (1716–84) was born in Kema, a suburb of Osaka. Later in life he took the surname Yosa. After Bashō died, as I mentioned earlier, the art of writing hokku again got lost in rules and over-sophistication. Buson, who lived about the time of Bach and Handel, was an exception to this degeneration in the art of hokku writing; in fact, he is now considered second only to Bashō as the greatest hokku poet.

Just as Bashō had restored hokku to a pure form, so Buson also brought hokku to another flowering after its period of deterioration following Bashō's death. Mukashi o Ima quotes Buson as saying, "I shall seek only for the elegant simplicity and sensitivity of old master Bashō and restore haiku to what it was in the ancient days." Buson was the center of the Return to Bashō Movement, and his group built a meeting house called *Bashō-an* (Bashō's Hut).

When Buson was twenty, he went to Edo (Tokyo) to study painting and there became Hayano Hajin's disciple and, for a time, secretary. Hayano Hajin had been a student of Takarai Kikaku, a disciple of Bashō. Buson spent his youth painting and writing hokku. He became established as an artist before becoming known as a haijin. He painted well and wrote of his paintings, "None of these pieces is ordinary. As for haiku-style brush paintings, there is nobody who can match me. This is a matter that I would not tell anyone else, only to you I confide it." This quote is from a letter to his dealer. His haiga include eleven scenes illustrating Bashō's *The Narrow Road to the Deep North*, which he undertook because of his veneration of Bashō.

After 1771 he began calling himself Yahantei (Mr. Midnight Pavilion) and later added "o," Yahan-o, to indicate "old" and also "master." Little is known of Buson's life. He frequented the theater and even acted occasionally, drank with friends, and consorted with *maiko* (apprentice geisha) and geisha. When he was about forty-five, he married and had a daughter. He was a lay Buddhist priest and spent many years in temples. He could support his family as a painter and so did not have to teach and correct haiku, and he was very contemptuous of those who did. "These days, those who dominate the haikai world peddle their different styles, ridicule and slander everyone else, and puff themselves up with the title of master." He was never as melancholy or as philosophical as Bashō, but was concerned with everyday people, whom he painted as well as wrote about. Unlike Bashō's spiritual and serious haiku, Buson's haiku were romantic, moody, sensual, and very painterly in quality.

He stated, "The essence of haikai is to use ordinary words and yet to become separate from the ordinary." He also advised, "Use the commonplace to escape the commonplace." Other Buson's sayings include: "Take all the streams into your water bag and keep them and choose for yourself what is good and use it for your purposes. Think for yourself about what you have inside yourself"; "What you want to acquire, you should dare to acquire"; "It is quite unusual to have a second chance to materialize your desire."

Nearly three thousand of Buson's haiku still exist, many of them using the form of internal comparison. Here is one of my favorites that I quoted earlier:

> mi ni shimu ya   a penetrating chill;
> naki tsuma no kushi wo   the comb of my long dead wife
> neya ni fumu   underfoot in the bedroom

It is not just the comb's teeth that penetrate Buson, but the cold because of his lost love. In reality, his wife was still alive when he wrote this poem, which, when I learned of it, certainly modified my enthusiasm for the haiku.

Here is Buson's last poem:

> shiraume
> ni akaru yo bakari
> to narinikeri

> *with white plum blossom*
> *this night to the first light of dawn*
> *is turning*

ISSA

Born in 1763, about the time of the Napoleonic wars, in Kashiwabara, a mountain village in what is now Nagano Prefecture, Kobayashi Tataro, also known as Kobayashi Nobuyuki, lived until 1827. He adopted the name Issa — a cup of tea (*ichi* meaning "one" and *cha* meaning "tea") — since he characterized his life as similar to that of the ephemeralness of froth on a cup of Japanese tea.

Neither a sensualist like Buson nor a Zen practitioner with the detachment of Bashō, Issa is my favorite haijin of the classical period. Issa was a human being of deep compassion, perhaps because his own life was very tragic. His mother died when he was three, and he was brought up by a stepmother who rejected him. His stepmother dressed him in shabby clothes, and the other children wouldn't play with him. It is thought that this tragic poem about his childhood was written years later when remembering his lonely early years:

> ware to kite
> asobeya oya no
> nai suzume

> *come over to me*
> *let's play together*
> *motherless sparrow*

At fifteen he left home and went to Edo (Tokyo). He returned home from time to time partly because he loved his village and partly because he was the first son and so stood to inherit land, but he was never really accepted. Meanwhile he had become a fine haijin. Like Bashō, he traveled widely and wore the robes of a Buddhist priest. When he was fifty, he returned home, married, and had five children, all of whom died young. His wife and young children all died in poverty. He married again, and then a third time, at which time his house burned down and, at the age of sixty-four, he moved into a friend's go-down (a building where family treasures are stored). He died of a stroke, leaving a wife and unborn daughter.

This haiku was written following the death of a young daughter:

tsuyu-no yo-no	*a dew-drop world*
tsuyu-no yo nagara	*though a dew-drop world*
sarinagara	*and yet . . .*

In the more than twenty thousand haiku that Issa wrote, beggars, warlords, frogs, and fleas were images used with equal interest, viewing everything as Buddha's Heaven, despite the many tragedies in his life. Issa's haiku are very accessible to the ordinary person. He loved to introduce surprise images in his haiku, such as a swallow flying out of the nostril of a Buddha statue or flower blossoms in the mud. He often addressed the animal he was writing about directly in his haiku. Robert Hass viewed many of his haiku as poor, but when it comes to compassion for the world's sufferings, there was no haijin like him, I feel:

yare utsu na	oh! don't swat it
hae ga te wo suru	the fly is wringing its hands
ashi wo suru	wringing its feet

His childlike haiku use everyday language and hold much
sympathy for animal and human alike. One of his last haiku
is my favorite:

tarai kara	from washbasin
tarai ni utsuru	to washbasin changing
chimpunkan	all is nonsense!

David Lanoue, the Issa authority, tells me that all evidence
points to this haiku not being written by Issa. Henderson
claims it was. Either way, I love it, and will let it sit
attributed to Issa, until I hear otherwise.

This next haiku is said to be the last poem of Issa's and was
found under the pillow of the bed on which he died:

there are thanks to be given:
this snow on the bed quilt —
it too is from Heaven.

CHIYO-NI

One doesn't hear much about women and haiku
historically, although nowadays in Japan, the majority
of haijin are women. During the Edo period (1694–1867),
women could only take part in the haiku world via a
male relative or husband. Probably the most famous
female haijin was Kaga no Chiyo, born in 1703 in Matto,
a small town in what is now Ishikawa Prefecture. I

particularly like her work because of its simplicity and sincerity.

Chiyo came from a family whose business was scroll-mounting, so from an early age, Chiyo was familiar with calligraphy, painting, and poetry. Chiyo-ni, Chiyo the nun, as she was later known, was a precocious child, and it is reported that she composed her first haiku when six years old. Her father recognised her talent and sent her to work with Hansui, a haiku master. Not only would he be able to encourage her writing, but also her painting and her learning of Chinese script, an unusual ability in women at that time. Later she studied with Shiko, one of Bashō's disciples.

Her most outstanding feature was her humbleness; she sought criticism of her haiku from masters long after she was a master herself. She didn't seek fame in Edo (Tokyo) or establish a school; she lived a simple life of extraordinary generosity to others. It is not known whether she ever married or bore children, although Leon Zolbrod claims that she did bear a child and lost it, and that she had a husband, but was left a widow. Some of her haiku are very sensual and imply that she had experienced emotional attachments, as in the haiku I quoted earlier:

tombo-tsuri   my dragon-fly hunter
kyō wa doko made   where has he wandered today
itta yara   I wonder?

She became a nun when she was fifty-two. As a nun, she was outside the caste system and so could travel freely and meet other poets, particularly male poets. Remember, women were forbidden to associate with males outside their own family.

It is told that Chiyo, then already an excellent haiku writer, went to her master and demanded to be given instructions on how she could write a haiku that was truly inspirational. He gave her the subject of "cuckoo," an ordinary enough one. What was she to do with that? She tried many times and almost despaired. One night she concentrated so hard on the theme that dawn broke before she realized she had been up all night. She wrote:

Hototogisu	*"cuckoo, cuckoo"*
Hototogisu tote	*all night long*
Akenikeri	*dawn already!*

Her master thought it one of the finest haiku ever written on the subject of the cuckoo because it genuinely expressed her feelings. Suzuki says that Chiyo "for the first time realized that a haiku, as long as it is a work of poetical creativity, ought to be an expression of one's inner feelings altogether devoid of the sense of ego." Patricia Donegan informs us that the above story is apocryphal, but it so aptly represents a Zen haiku that I still find it useful. Chiyo-ni had two collections of her poetry published, a rare thing for a woman. My favorite haiku of Chiyo-ni's, and her best known, is:

asagao ya	*morning glory—*
tsurube torarete	*the well-bucket entangled*
morai mizu	*I ask for water*

—translated by Patricia Donegan

Her advice — "Appreciate each moment; that's all there really is." Here is Chiyo-ni's death haiku:

tsuki mo mite	*having seen the moon*
ware wa kono yo o	*I now say to the world*
kashiku kana	*"Farewell"*

Kashiku was the way women ended their letters, and here, in this haiku, a letter is used as a metaphor for life. She died in 1775.

SHIKI

Masaoka Tsunenori (1867–1902) was born in Matsuyama a year before the Meiji Restoration, a new beginning for Japan, and a new beginning for haiku. Tsunenori was sometimes called Noboru and later adopted the name Shiki. Shiki was a bird in the cuckoo family that, it is said, in order to get a certain quality in its singing had to sing until it coughed blood. Shiki had tuberculosis and spat blood, so he found that pseudonym suitable:

Ganjitsu ya	New Year's Day
karegiku nokoru	dead chrysanthemums still
niwa no saki	at the garden's edge

Shiki started his career by denigrating Bashō — certainly a useful way to leap onto center stage in the haiku world — by claiming that four-fifths of Bashō's haiku were mediocre. As mentioned earlier, Bashō never claimed he wrote a high percentage of good haiku. Bashō almost became deified, but Shiki turned to Buson, rather than Bashō, as a model because Buson's haiku were "colorful and startling." Shiki declared seven or eight out of every ten haiku by Buson were excellent!

What Shiki really wanted to do was to free haiku from the strict rules of word usage and subject matter that had once more ossified it and made writing haiku an elaborate game. As Ueda states, haiku had become "trite, pretentious, and devoid of emotional appeal." Ironically enough, Shiki's austere, fresh haiku eventually set him alongside Bashō, Buson, and Issa as one of the four keystone masters of haiku.

Shiki and his group expounded their principles in an article in *Nippon* in 1896: "Appeal directly to the emotions, choose fresh motifs, abhor wordiness, words can come from any source (even Western) so long as they harmonize, the merit of a haiku rests solely on the poet (or rather the poem), irrespective of the 'school' he belongs to."

Shiki thought haiku should be based on shasei, sketches from natural life, and divided them into two types: Buson's haiku represented objective shasei and Bashō's represented subjective shasei. Shasei, as a term for haiku, means direct seeing into nature and is a spontaneous moment of perception and experience. Blyth said it was a delineation of nature. The term shasei comes from the practice of direct painting from nature or a sketch from life, as a painter painting *en plein air* might record the immediacy of what he or she is seeing, or as someone seeing nature through fresh eyes, as a child might. This was Shiki's approach. Henderson points out that for the translator, "the 'picture poems' are very hard because one must be familiar with every object in the picture." Shiki thought the three essential elements of haiku were shasei (sketching from nature), objective description, and juxtaposition (harmonizing antitheses):

nan to iu	I do not know
tori ka shiranedo	what bird it was, but
umi no eda	the spray of plum blossom

— translated by Blyth

Although the word haiku had been around for many years, Shiki proposed it be used for the hokku, allowing it to be considered as an entirely separate poetry form and not as an introductory verse. As Ueda interprets Shiki, "A good poem will always be new in its motif, unhackneyed in its material, uninhibited in its vocabulary, and therefore direct in its emotional appeal and fresh in its overall impression. That is the haiku as different from the hokku of old":

nakihito no	the dead soldier's
mukuro wo kakuse	corpse hidden
haru no kusa	spring grasses

Nevertheless, although haiku after Shiki may not be uniformly brilliant, Henderson feels the surprisingly high level of good haiku is partly due to Shiki's influence. Henderson considers Shiki more important as an innovator than as a haijin. Shiki wrote eighteen thousand haiku. This is my favorite Shiki haiku, which I quoted earlier:

kaerimireba	looking back
yukiaishi	the man I greeted just now
hito kasumi keri	is lost in mist

And another favorite of mine:

yuku ware ni	for I who go
todomari nare ni	for you who stay
aki futatsu	two autumns

Blyth says of this haiku that "the whole of life is given here, our meetings, our partings, the world of nature we each live in, different yet the same."

Shiki wrote three haiku on his death bed:

hechima saite	sponge gourd has bloomed
tanno tsumarishi	choked by phlegm
hotoke kana	a departed soul

tan itto	gallons of phlegm
hechima no mizu mo	even the gourd water
maniawazu	couldn't clear it up

ototoi no	the night before
hechima no mizu mo	yesterday's gourd water
torazarikithey	didn't get it either

SEISHI

Seishi (1901–94) was born as Yamaguchi Chikahiko (later Yamaguchi Seishi.) He was a student of Takahama Kyoshi, who was a student of Shiki.

"Contemporary haiku began with Yamaguchi Seishi and his works," states Azuma Kyōzō. Seishi founded and managed the monthly periodical *Tenrō*, and went through many thousands of haiku every week for the Asahi newspaper (can you imagine a North American newspaper having a poetry consultant!), as well as giving many lectures.

He expanded subject matter to cover urban life and made it modern by not always using the soft "singing birds and flowers" kind of haiku, but by introducing hard industrial images. "The material should be new and the sentiment deep," he stated. It is thought that *kogarashi* (chilly winds) in the following haiku refers to the kamikaze pilots, who of course, also never returned:

umi ni dete	once over the sea
kogarashi kaeru	chilly winds can no longer
tokoro nashi	return home again

His essential element is juxtaposition — putting the seasonal phrase as an anchor next to a present, but contrasting aspect of human nature. He quotes Mallarmé, "Since objects are already in existence, it is not necessary to create them. All we have to do is grasp the relationships among them."

Of the Atomic Bomb Dome, he wrote:

shunkan ni	in an instant
wankyoku no tetsu	twisted iron
kanzarashi	exposed to the cold

My favorite Seishi haiku:

natsukasa ni	at the summer grasses
kikansha no sharin	the wheels of an engine
kite tomaru	come to a stop

and

sakura saku   before the cherry blossom
mae yori kōki   the branches are misted
tachikomete   with a pink haze

To celebrate Seishi's contribution to haiku writing, his fans have put his haiku on stone monuments throughout Japan, even one on top of Mt. Fuji.

Shiki's main disciple, Hekigodō, freed the haiku even further until it became almost a *vers libre* with a season word. Later, Kyoshi returned haiku to its more traditional form, but encouraged many new haijin by his teaching and criticism. While the haiku of Natsume Sōseki, Takihama Kyoshi, Kawahigashi Hekigodō, Ogiwara Seisensui, Murakami Kijō (the twentieth-century Issa), Iida Dakotsu (the modern Bashō), and other poets of the early and mid-twentieth century can be found in translation in *Modern Japanese Haiku* by Makoto Ueda, Yamaguchi Seishi seems to be the most frequently translated of this period.

WHY WRITE HAIKU?

WHY BOTHER WITH HAIKU IN THE TWENTY-FIRST CENTURY, when so many other things can occupy your time?

♦ As Clark Strand so beautifully says, "it restores balance." Writing haiku literally brings you to your senses, grounds you, and helps you see things from a wider perspective, from a correcting position.

♦ Recording haiku alerts the haijin to a greater awareness of the universe and the mystery of the relatedness between seemingly unrelated things. Haiku helps you appreciate the interdependence of all things and the importance of the reactions your behavior may have on all things, organic or not.

♦ The electric light removed the difference between night and day, and heating and cooling systems have evened out the seasons, therefore haiku plays an important role in reminding us that we are still a part of nature ourselves and subject to the cycles that all manifestation goes through.

♦ Bashō's quote is relevant here: "reinvigoration of the heart through communion with nature."

♦ Haiku are the penetration of concepts in order to become more thoroughly acquainted personally with the truth of things as they really are . . . the "suchness" of things. Grass, moon, waves are ordinary things, yet experiencing them by writing haiku can, at the deepest level, bring us face to face with truth by using feelings and intuition rather than intellect — the grass-ness, the moon-ness, the wave-ness of things. This understanding seems to me to be the foundation of haiku. Haiku present the mysteries in a way that reverberates with the deepest level of our beings. And it is all ordinary! Haiku express "when the finite becomes conscious of the infinite residing within it," as said by Daisetz T. Suzuki.

♦ Haiku writing makes you more conscious of the words you choose in expressing yourself and the clarity with which you can communicate.

♦ Writing haiku helps you appreciate the wonder of ordinary things and ordinary days.

♦ Haiku can make you curious about Japanese culture and the subtle sensibilities that are displayed by its master craftspeople, writers, and artists.

♦ Haiku writing trains you to see with directness and lack of guile, as only some children (and some very old people) can.

♦ Haiku keep you anchored in the present rather than brooding on the past or worrying about the future. Jane Reichhold felt that writing haiku is a discipline and that if you are interested in haiku, you are seeking more discipline in your life.

♦ One doesn't need money or qualifications to write haiku, just pencil and paper and sometimes not even that:

no paper
I write a haiku
on a shell

It is good to look on all things as in progress: unfolding, growing, decaying, dying, being reborn, hating, loving, spirals of energy . . . constantly shimmering. A haiku is a pause, a cross-section, a still. Maybe what we think of as the pulsating energy of life is a series of stills, just as a cartoon is. Animation is a set of stillnesses. The haijin sees the stillness in the animation. Not every time, of course, but when the heart stops in admiration, a stillness has been captured. Yet even as it is captured and pinned down on three lines, it has escaped and vanished into the next stillness, the next animation.

APPENDIX ONE

HAIKU TIPS — A SUMMING UP

HAIKU ARE MAYBES, NOT CERTAINTIES. HINTS ARE BETTER than overloads.

* Haiku writing is about catching the moment, so haiku are always written in the present tense. They tell what, when, and where something is taking place. One moment in time captured.

* Haiku are poems of the senses — what you are seeing, hearing, smelling, touching, tasting.

* Do not express any emotions directly in haiku. No "this is so wonderful," no "what a shame!" What you are aiming for is to show the reader what has caused your emotions. If you do this well, the reader will immediately intuit what you are feeling.

* Because you are writing about one moment, you don't have time to think of metaphors and similes. You are not telling me how this is like that, you are telling me how this is like this.

* 5, 7, 5 syllables refers to the writing of haiku in Japanese. In English, haiku are usually written 2 beats, 3 beats, 2 beats, or short line, longer line, short line. Experimental haiku of one line or using very few words are occasionally seen. The spirit of the haiku is more important than the syllable count or number of words used.

♦ There are no capitals used in haiku unless you are using a capitalized noun. The moment springs from the past and leaves to make room for the future. Starting with a capital letter and finishing with a full stop would deny giving the brief flash of the moment we are trying to capture its setting.

♦ Haiku usually consist of two contrasting or complimentary linked images — for example, a near one and a far one; a big one and a little one; a new object and an old one; etc. The juxtaposition and linking of the two parts is the essence of haiku writing. The pause between the images is often shown by an em dash (—) or ellipse (. . .).

♦ As you have few words to set the scene and tell us what you are sensing, there is no room for useless descriptions such as "pretty" or "ugly"; "good" or "bad." There is no room for judgmental statements, so choose your adjectives carefully, if you use them at all. In haiku each word must carry its weight,

♦ When it comes to subject matter for haiku, again it is dispassionate — feces and butterflies are equally acceptable.

♦ Stop the chattering mind and make room for the haiku to pop in.

♦ Be specific. Don't use "trees," "flowers." Tell us what trees and which flowers. However, don't be so specific that what you are writing about is only known locally or to a few people. This is particularly true of the seasonal words you choose to use. Haiku is about sharing. In classical Japanese haiku, because the country was relatively homogenous, allusions to previous writings would immediately be recognized. Allusions are rare in haiku written in English.

♦ Don't use academic words or obscure words. Don't be clever. Haiku is about the everyday.

♦ Show, don't tell. Telling involves the intellect, showing uses the senses.

♦ Contemplate nature as closely as you can, even if you live in the city. You are relating natural cycles with your life cycle.

♦ Rhyme gets in the way and is usually too clever. Haiku don't need cleverness, they need simplicity.

♦ Get out of the way so you can closely identify with your subject without letting your emotions, judgments, and intellectual ideas get in the way.

♦ Read, read, read. Write, write, write.

APPENDIX TWO

EXERCISES FOR HAIKU WRITING

As I quoted before, Bashō pointed out that "a haiku should be written as quickly as a swordsman wields his sword or a tree-cutter his axe." Both swordsman and woodsman need to practice their skills, and so does the writer of haiku.

♦ Write haiku being aware that you are answering the following questions — when are you writing this? what are you sensing? and where is this taking place? Three questions, three lines. This should give you a strong seasonal image which is somehow linked intuitively to human nature.

♦ Write haiku being aware that you are recording something passing, something eternal, and a link. As Kodaira Takahashi states, "While taking hold of the present moment, haiku must grasp with the eye of the spirit the invisible relationships existing among objects lost in time and space." Robert Hass also speaks of the tension "between the comfort of magical, cyclical time and the self-erasing linear time."

♦ Take a haiku walk, writing rapid 3-liners recording what you see. Out of all of them, one will be a beauty.

♦ Try for the internal comparison — one subject anchors the haiku in the season, the other compares it to something in human nature. *Niku isshō* (two phrases, one poem). This usually produces an interesting haiku.

♦ Make a list of words associated with each season for the area you live in.

♦ Blyth instructed that if you want to point out the moon and your finger is covered in rings, you must take off the rings so that the viewer can concentrate on the moon. So make sure no unnecessary words are present to impede the reader resonating with your haiku.

♦ Try to observe dispassionately, without judgment.

♦ Subjects deemed "distasteful" by some, are as suitable as "cherry blossoms" and "swans" in the writing of haiku.

If you would like more excellent haiku-priming exercises, check these websites:

Bare Bones School of Haiku [http://www.ahapoetry.com/haiartjr.htm]

[http://www.graceguts.com/workshops/haiku-workshops]

BIBLIOGRAPHY

Akmakjian, Hiag. *Snow Falling from a Bamboo Leaf.* Santa
Barbara, California: Capra Press, 1979.

Amann, Eric. *Wordless Poem.* Haiku Society of Canada,
1969.

Blyth, R. H. *A History of Haiku* (in two volumes).Tokyo:
Hokuseido, 1964.

Bowers, Faubion, ed. *The Classic Tradition of Haiku.* Dover
Thrift Edition, 1996.

Brown, J. C. *Senryū: Poems and People.* Rutland, Vermont:
Tuttle, 1991.

Donegan, Patricia and Yoshie Ishibashi. *Chiyo-ni.* Singapore:
Tuttle, 1998.

Emrich, Jeanne. *The Haiku Habit.* Minnesota: Lone Egret
Press, 1996.

Bashō. *The Narrow Road to the Deep North.* Translated by
Sam Hamill. Boston: Shambhala, 1991.

Hass, Robert, ed. *The Essential Haiku.* Hopewell, New
Jersey: Ecco Press, 1994.

Henderson, Harold G. *Haiku in English.* Rutland, Vermont:
Charles E. Tuttle, 1967.

———. *The Bamboo Broom.* Folcroft, Pennsylvania: Folcroft
Library Editions, 1971.

———. *An Introduction to Haiku.* Rutland, Vermont:
Charles E. Tuttle, 1958.

Higginson, William. *The Haiku Handbook: How to Write,
Share, and Teach Haiku.* Toronto: McGraw-Hill, 1985.

Hoffmann, Yoel. *Japanese Death Poems.* Tokyo: Tuttle, 1986.

Lanoue, David G., trans. *Cup of Tea Poems.* Freemont,
California: Asia Humanities Press, 1979.

Mayhew, Lenore, trans. *Monkey's Raincoat*. Rutland,
    Vermont: Tuttle, 1993.

Reichhold, Jane. *Writing and Enjoying Haiku*. Tokyo:
    Kodansha, 2002.

Ross, Bruce, ed. *Haiku Moment*. Rutland, Vermont: Tuttle,
    1993.

Strand, Clark. *Seeds from a Birch Tree*. New York: Hyperion,
    1997.

Ueda, Makoto. *Modern Japanese Haiku*. University of
    Toronto Press, 1976.

van den Heuvel, Cor, ed. *The Haiku Anthology*, New York:
    W. W. Norton, 1999.

Wakan, Naomi Beth. *Haiku — one breath poetry*. California:
    Heian International, 1993.

Zolbrod, Leon. *Haiku Painting*. Tokyo: Kodansha, 1982.

LIST OF HAIJIN MENTIONED IN THE TEXT

Akutegawa, Ryūnosuke (1892–1927)—haijin and short
story writer
Amann, Eric (1934–2016)—one of the founders of Haiku
Canada
Andreyev, Alexey—leading Russian haiku writer; and
commentator on the haiku scene
Arima, Akito—nuclear physicist, politician, and haijin

Baker, Winona—leading Canadian haijin
Bashō, Matsuo (1644–94)—leading haijin
Blofeld, John (1913–87)—Buddhist scholar
Blyth, R. H. (1898–1964)—author of the four-volume
Haiku
Britton, Dorothy (1922–2015)—composer, author, poet

Chiyo-ni (1703–75)—leading female haijin
Clausen, Tom—American haijin
Cobb, David—noted haijin; one of the founders of the
British Haiku Society

Doeff, Hendrik (1777–1835)—first Westerner known to
have written haiku
Donegan, Patricia—author of *Chiyo-ni: Woman Haiku
Master*; promoter of haiku as an awareness practice
Drevniok, Betty—past president of Haiku Canada; has a
prize named after her

Frampton, Alice—Canadian/American haijin; co-
founder of Seabeck Haiku Getaway

Gorman, LeRoy — Canadian haijin
Gyōdai (1732–93) — haijin

Hachiemon, Karai (Senryū) (1718–90) — haijin
Hajin Hayano — haikai master
Hamill, Sam (1943–2018) — American poet
Hass, Robert — United States Poet Laureate 1995–97
Henderson, Harold G. (1889–1974) — cofounded the
    Haiku Society of America
Higginson, William J. (1938–2008) — American poet and
    translator
Hisago, Sugita (1890–1946) — female haijin
Hoover, Tom — American writer
Howard, Dorothy — former president of Haiku Canada

Ichiki, Tadao — Japanese writer
Iida, Dakotsu (1885–1962) — the modern Bashō
Ishida, Hakyō (1913–69) — haijin

Kacian, Jim — former editor of *Frogpond*; founder of Red
    Moon Press
Kaneko, Tōta (1919–2018) — honorary chair of the
    Modern Haiku Association
Katō, Shūson (1905–93) — haijin
Kawabata, Bōsha (1897–1941) — haijin
Kawahigashi, Hekigodō (1873–1937) — haijin
Kikaku, Takarai (1661–1707) — haijin
Kobayashi, Issa (1763–1867) — major haijin
Kolompar, Angelika — Canadian haijin

MacRury, Carole — American haijin and haiga artist
McMurray, David — curator of Asahi Haiku Column
Masaoka, Shiki (1867–1902) — major haijin

Murakami, Kijō (1865–1938)—haijin

Ogiwara, Seisensui (1884–1976)—haijin
Ōnishi, Tatsuō—haijin
Onitsura, Uejima (1660–1783)—haijin

Pizzarelli, Alan—haijin; well-known exponent of senryū

Quammen, David—science writer

Reichhold, Jane (1937–2016)—wrote extensively about haiku on and off the Web

Sato, Kazuo—former director of the international division of the Museum of Haiku Literature
Sōjō, Hino (1901–56)—haijin
Sōseki, Natsume (1867–1916)—Japanese poet and novelist
Speiss, Robert (1921–2002)—former editor of *Modern Haiku*
Strand, Clark—former senior editor of *Tricycle* magazine
Sugita, Hisajo (1890–1946)—noted female haijin
Suzuki, Daisetz (1870–1966)—writer on Zen and Japanese culture
Swede, George—major Canadian haijin, co-founded Haiku Canada

T'ai, Wei (eleventh century)—Song dynasty poet
Takahashi, Kodaira—haijin
Takiguchi, Susumu—founder and president of the World Haiku Club
Takihama, Kyoshi (1874–1959)—haijin

Talbot, Norman — poet; former professor of English at Newcastle University

Uchida, Sonō — Japanese poet
Ueda, Makoto — author of books on renka, tanka and haiku

van den Heuvel, Cor — past president of the Haiku Society of America

Watanabe, Kazan (1793–1841) — painter
Welch, Michael Dylan — major North American haijin

Yamaguchi, Seishi (1901–94) — haijin
Yamaguchi, Tazuo — Japanese / American poet
Yarrow, Ruth — American poet and teacher of environmental studies
Yasuda, Kenneth (1914–2002) — author of *Japanese Haiku*
Yosa, Buson (1716–84) — leading haijin

Zolbrod, Leon (1930–91) — professor at the University of British Columbia; authority on Haiga and Noh

HAIKU SOURCES

Websites are notoriously ephemeral. These sites were "live" at the time of publication:

http://contemporaryhaibunonline.com
http://www.haibuntoday.com
http://prunejuice.wordpress.com
http://shamrockhaiku.webs.com
http://www.theheronsnest.com
http://www.haikuworld.org
http://www.hsa-haiku.org
Haiku Society of America
http://www.ahapoetry.com
Jane Reichold's Bare Bones School of Haiku
http://www.bregengemme.net/chrysanthemum.php
http://www.worldhaikureview.org
http://www.modernhaiku.org
website of *Modern Haiku,* also available in print
http://sites.google.com/site/graceguts
Any reference that points to pieces on haiku by Michael Dylan Welch will be very useful; he is a brilliant, sensitive interpreter and writer of haiku.

PRINT PUBLICATIONS

Asahi Evening News, "Haikuist network"
  5-3-2T Sukiji, Chuo-ku, Tokyo 104-11 Japan
Blithe Spirit, The Journal of the British Haiku Society,
  12 Eliot Vale, Black Heath, London SE3 0UW
Bottle Rockets Press, publisher of haiku, senryu & other
  small poems **http://www.bottlerocketspress.com/**
chrysanthemum magazine **http://www.
  bregengemme.net/chrysanthemum.php**
Daily Yomiuri, "Haiku Section"(newspaper)
  1-7-1 Otemachi, Chiyoda-ku, Tokyo 100-55, Japan
Frogpond, The Journal of the Haiku Society of America
  http://www.hsa-haiku.org/frogpond
Haiku Canada Review **http://www.haikucanada.
  org/home/publications.php**
Mainichi (newspaper)
  1-1-1, Hitotsubashi, Chiyoda, Tokyo
Modern Haiku **http://www.modernhaiku.org**

HAIGA SITES

http://www.dailyhaiga.org
http://www.haigaonline.com
http://www.oston.shawbiz.ca Jim Swift's excellent
  haiga site

ABOUT THE AUTHOR

 NAOMI BETH WAKAN is the Inaugural Poet Laureate of Nanaimo, British Columbia, Canada, and the Inaugural Honorary Ambassador for the Federation of British Columbia Writers. She has published over fifty books, including the American Library Association selection, *Haiku — one breath poetry* (Heian International). Her latest titles are *The Way of Tanka* and *Poetry That Heals*, both from Shanti Arts. Wakan is a member of The League of Canadian Poets, Haiku Canada, and Tanka Canada. She lives on Gabriola Island, British Columbia, with her husband, the sculptor, Elias Wakan.

www.naomiwakan.com

SHANTI ARTS
nature · art · spirit

Please visit us on online

to browse our entire book catalog,

including additional poetry collections and fiction,

books on travel, nature, healing, art,

photography, and more.

www.shantiarts.com

CPSIA information can be obtained
at www.ICGtesting.com
Printed in the USA
LVHW012130210519
618618LV00017B/1155/P